W9-DED-540

A THOUSAND DEER

Four Generations of Hunting and the Hill Country

RICK BASS

UNIVERSITY OF TEXAS PRESS ⩔ AUSTIN

Requests for permission to reproduce material from this work should be sent to:
Permissions
University of Texas Press
P.O. Box 7819
Austin, TX 78713-7819
www.utexas.edu/utpress/about/bpermission.html

The paper used in this book meets the minimum requirements of
ANSI/NISO Z39.48-1992 (R1997) (Permanence of Paper). ∞

Library of Congress Cataloging-in-Publication Data

Bass, Rick, 1958–
A thousand deer : four generations of hunting
and the Hill Country / Rick Bass.
p.   cm. — Ellen and Edward Randall Series
ISBN 978-0-292-73795-2 (cloth : alk. paper)
1. Bass, Rick, 1958– 2. Big game hunters—Texas—Biography.
3. Deer hunting—Texas—History. 4. Deer hunting—Texas—Anecdotes.
I. Title.
SK17.B38A3 2012
799.2'765092—dc23 [B]
2012020594

CONTENTS

A THOUSAND DEER

MY NATURALIST MOTHER

AS WITH THE BEST OF GIFTS, the recipient did not even recognize the gift as such until long years after the giving. I'm pretty sure that when I was growing up in Houston in the 1960s my mother did not keep a tally, an internal registry, called *Nature Quota* or *Things to do Outside Each Day for the Betterment of My Children*. Instead, paying attention to nature—and I think she would have defined the term "nature" as any and all living things beyond one's self—was simply how she lived her life. She did so with a passion and vitality that was contagious, whether commenting on whatever bird had just arrived to spray seed from the backyard feeder, or naming the different gray and fox squirrels that patrolled the suburban yards and littered the driveways and sidewalks with sharply gnawed fragments of hickory nuts that pierced the feet of barefooted walkers. She supported enthusiastically my boyhood predilection for keeping as pets whatever bayou creatures I could capture—slender grass snakes, bewitching with their emerald sheen, giant bullfrog pollywogs, their bulbous heads seeming to suggest a cetacean intelligence, prehistoric soft-shelled turtles, pancake-shaped with pale bellies and periscope necks. Freshwater crawfish, nine-lined skinks, box turtles, catfish, topwater minnows, ram's horn snails: it must have seemed that at some point every creature in the kingdom of life had passed through and lived temporarily in our home, and from this parade, my mother impressed upon me the habit not just of looking beyond one's self, but also of being stimulated and enthused by what the world—the natural world—had to offer.

This was not a message or ethos that was preached by her, but instead, one she lived by example; it was simply how she inhabited the world—one of the ways she loved the world—and when you love something, you want to share it. This is an obvious but important distinction: the fact that she didn't arise each day with a parenting checklist, but instead brought me to nature more organically, without the pressure of agenda or correct or incorrect answer.

Nature—wild nature—was going away then, too, as it is now, but I think we lived in that last time of grace before the full foreknowledge of the rates of extinctions and loss had become a part of our consciousness. Folks like myself are sometimes guilty of saying things like *I wish I'd been born a hundred years earlier*, or *How I would have liked to have seen this country when it was young and whole and strong*—but the truth is I can't really complain. I had it pretty good.

In retrospect, from a natural history perspective, I think I got to inhabit the last good childhood unfreighted by that degree of awareness of loss—that she and I got to inhabit it together—and I'm grateful to her, and consider myself lucky, even if possessing also the bittersweet guilt of the survivor. I must confess that these days I do not always follow my mother's model, and when I show my daughters some aspect of nature, whether sublime or subtle, I often do so with that confusion of self-awareness: wondering, is this something—a warbler, a certain glacier, the sound of a snipe in spring—that they will be able to share with their children? Knowing, sometimes, that the answer well may be *Perhaps not*.

I understand or believe that there are genetic dispositions—pre-existing circuitries that might illuminate in the midst of the natural world—and that surely my mother's (and my father's) and mine were wired from birth for such ignition. But brain research is showing that equally powerful neural pathways can be built in the brain for such things even if none exist at birth. With regard to my own naturalist's upbringing, then, I believe I got a double dose. Surely there were days of my suburban childhood that passed without some contact with nature, but if such days existed, they have been scoured clean in my memory by the eradicating winds of time.

What I do remember is the excitement of discovering any animal's tracks in the backyard, and of how we would spend hours mixing up a plaster of paris cast, and, subsequently, a wax imprint. Decades later, I would see such plaster imprints in the offices of wildlife biologists—casts from the immense feet of grizzlies, wolves, mountain lions—and I would feel a kind of immediate kinship, irrespective that my own childhood quarry had been basset hound, opossum, raccoon. The specificity of detail preserved in those casts was no less present in the filigree of pad, the wrinkled delicate underfeet of the suburban raccoon than in the tufted toepads of Canadian lynx.

What it was like, back then—I remember this now—is that there was a glow that would heat up and incandesce in my mind when I saw these things, and when I engaged with them and with that outside, natural world, which was only half a step farther than the interior life of my mind.

Back then, I was not aware of such illumination—the blaze of those existing pathways surging with the recognition of attachment, the match and fit of their desire and the sculpted world beyond, as well as the burning of new pathways across the not-yet mapped territory of my boyhood brain—but looking back now, I can see that that was how it must have been.

I am not willing to admit yet that my middle-aged brain has grown darker or sealed over with the plaque and detritus of sediment, minutiae, and, perhaps worst of all, the dross of familiarity, when in truth there is still so much in the world that by all rights should be every bit as mysterious to me now as it was then. In the looking-back, though, it seems to me that in my vision of that boy-in-nature, I see the light of his mind glowing even in the darkness of nightfall, lit like a burning lantern.

My mother would have been in her early thirties. Surely her own mind-in-nature was still glowing brightly then. Like the best of guides, she led me to places where those pathways lit up, and then stepped aside, allowing me my own discoveries, my own burnings, with the pleasure, perhaps, of the hunter-gatherer who shares his or her good fortune with others, or who brings a fellow hunter into a forest or a valley where the hunting is good.

NEARLY EVERY SATURDAY MORNING, after I had finished watching the early showing of *Bomba the Jungle Boy* or *Tarzan*, my mother would drive me way across town to the Museum of Natural History for the weekly Saturday lecture. The chief reptile guy for the zoo was Dr. John Werler, a kind of local Crocodile Hunter decades before such a niche found fascination with the general public. (Like many in his profession, Werler had on occasion been bitten by his quarry—usually a rattlesnake—but always, he survived.)

Sometimes the lectures would be about piranhas or Komodo dragons— other times, less exotic Texana, though no less fascinating: mockingbirds, wolf spiders, armadillos. I drank it in. This attentiveness was the fabric of my days. There were other components to my days, but nature—even suburban nature, which was the only nature I knew, beyond that of my imagination, and those itchy wilderness pathways not yet fully constructed in my mind— was always the touchstone of those days.

I want to be clear: my mother was not a science wonk. There was less science in those days, and it was less accessible. She was more of an observer and participant and also, more than anything, a daily celebrant. To use a most common cliché, it rubbed off on me. We were cut from the same cloth.

IT WAS MY FATHER who took me to wilder places. Since the early 1930s, he and his brother and my grandfather had leased a hunting camp on a thousand acres in the hardscrabble rocks and canyons of the Hill Country, up past Fredericksburg. It was a time before cedar and tourism had taken over the land, a time when grass fires still kept the cedar burned back, and the only land my family could afford to lease was the ragged land that nobody else wanted.

As rough and worthless as that country was to the economic models of the times, it was beautiful to us. Too rocky even for goats, and certainly possessing not enough soil for cattle or crops, it was a jumble of giant eroding granite boulders in the shapes of globes and rectangles and fantastic animals—a rhino, a camel, an Easter Island visage, a clenched fist—and the Comanches had revered it. Their flint knappings and arrowheads lay in the scree and granite chat aprons of the disintegrating hills, and it was not hard to imagine encampments of them, in the old days, sitting up in those boulders, building their fires, and making arrowheads with antler and stone.

My father took me up there a couple of times a year, driving long distances over rough ranch roads the last couple of hours, and even though in Houston I had sought out whatever wild little pockets of vacant lot woodland, cattle prairie, and oxbow bayou I could find at the farthest edge of the slowly expanding suburbs—in whose expansion, certainly, we were complicit—there was no comparison, in terms of wildness, between those city-edge pockets of thriving and somewhat disturbed nature, and the scale of ecological integrity I found in the Hill Country, back in the rocks and cactus, and so far—or so it seemed to me, a child—from the hand of man.

Back then, the Hill Country—the lease we called "the deer pasture"—a joke, for certainly, there was no pasture—was as wild to the ten- and twelve-year-old boy I was as would be Alaska's Brooks Range and Canada's Muskwa-Kechika, as an adult.

Wyoming's Wind River Range, Utah's Uintas, Colorado's San Juans, Montana's Bob Marshall Wilderness: it is all a question of scale. Certainly, a healthy earth needs these cores of big untouched country to help serve as wellsprings of vitality and integrity for those scattered distant archipelagos of mere "nature"—call it the managed pastoral, the domesticated living. But these smaller, more moderated contacts with nature—the sparrows, marsh rabbits, white-tailed deer—can also help by serving as a bridge back from where we are now, frazzled and confused, back to the touchstone of a larger and wilder landscape, where the brushstrokes of nature were and are bolder and more complex.

We would do well to remember, I think, that all the world was once wilderness—the world that shaped and sculpted our brains as well as our bodies, and our systems of logic. It was and remains the baseline, the foundation of whatever we choose to call "nature"—the place where all the rest of nature first came from. I was extraordinarily fortunate in my growing-up childhood, in the late 1950s and on through the 60s, in a place, Houston, that was decidedly no longer wild, to have both nature and wildness in my life: to have the daily example of my mother, as well as those farther trips with my father.

AGAIN, WHAT I REALIZE now was rare about my mother's embrace of suburban nature was the good fortune of my not viewing that embrace as either instruction or leave-taking. There was not that veil of impending sorrow that accompanies many of my own moments in nature these days, when I pause to consider the endgame, the underlying fundamentals. She walked in beauty all of her days, we wrote of her, after her too-early death in 1991, and the older I get, the more I realize what an accomplishment that is, in any age: seemingly the simplest thing in the world, yet paradoxically one of the easiest to forget.

Would I have loved the deep wilderness as much had my mother not loved our backyard nature so much? There is no telling. What I do believe is that it is a continuum, and that I couldn't be luckier. It might have been nice to grow up in Alaska, trapping beaver and sewing our clothes from caribou skin, but to have grown up in the petrochemical corridor of Houston, I couldn't have been luckier. When she heard the snow geese and Canada geese fly over at night in the fall and winter on their migrations to the Katy Prairie, she called us out onto the lawn to hear it. Nothing of the grand spectacle of the living escaped her notice or celebration. All the love of wildness in me that would grow later came, I think, in large part from my good fortune to have both parents, in different ways, willing to step toward nature and wildness, rather than away.

The point is not so much whether one choice, wilderness or the pastoral, is a substrate for the other, nor is one better than the other, but of how rich we are to still have both, to still have an opportunity for a sense of balance in lives that often feel cut-off and imbalanced—though cut off from what, we sometimes cannot even say.

My own personal view is that the rarest thing is the wilderness—that big country grows smaller every day—but that with a child, the smallest serving of nature is all that is required to ignite that lifelong relationship with what, for lack of better phrasing, we call "the natural world."

ONE MORE THOUGHT. I perceived—and still believe—that as a child, I existed in a time of bounty. I think our culture today understands that due to our horrific affluence and consumption, the world exists in a time of increasing paucity and diminishment. This is a situation that is aggravated by our increasing estrangement from the rhythms, pulses, and celebrations of our lives, and lives beyond our own.

It is with a bittersweet feeling that I remember those childhood days of plenty. There is often a phenomenon in nature where the peak of a system's productivity occurs not in the relative stasis of mid-range security and stability, but instead after the system has received its first major damage. The conifer that is struck by lightning summons all its energies to produce a greater crop of seed cones, casting them down onto the rich waiting ashes of the burn below.

It was like that, I know now, in the suburbs I inhabited at the edges of the prairie and woodland, where the bulldozers' first bladecuts and the tractors' first clawings had scratched that rich soil, summoning a more inspired outpouring of life from that initial disturbance.

Everywhere I looked there was a scurrying, with the bayou bottomland sending a diaspora into the newly colonized yards and gardens, as we and our houses and homes crept farther into the fraying edges of what had once been a great kingdom unto its own.

What I remember in particular, when I consider the bounty—the pulse of what I am tempted to call excess—are the toads. Every yard in our new subdivision had a sputtering little gaslight streetlamp, so that late at night in the summer after the sun had gone down, and the stars were silhouetting the tops of the tall pines, the streets of the new neighborhood each appeared to be like winding rivers of dull gold. The gaslights were intended to mimic the Victorian quality of merry old England—street names included the words "Windsor," "Brook," and "Glen"—but what the gaslights looked like to me were tiny campfires, candles in the wilderness.

And in the summer, moths and lacewings and June bugs swarmed the yellowpanes of those lights in a coming-and-going that was as perfect as the tides. Each afternoon the mosquito fogger would drive down the streets in his big tanker-truck, fumigating the neighborhood in a toxic glowing blue light, but still the insects came, night after night, not long after darkness first fell and the ever-burning streetlamps resumed their primacy in that suburban black.

Just as unfailingly, the toads gathered around the streetlamps like diners crowded around a great feast and waited, patiently it seemed, for the wing-burnished insects to collide mid-flight and tumble to the ground, or to damage their wings against the hot panes of the glass, or to simply become tired of flying and flutter to the ground for a while: a mistake.

These were big toads; they gorged every night, all night, on that bounty. I cannot describe to you how many there were. Not only did they crowd around every little streetlight that stippled those lanes through the forest, one-sixteenth of an acre at a time, they also filled the sidewalks and spilled out into the streets. They emerged at nightfall from beneath every stone in every garden, hopping through the lawns of newly shorn St. Augustine; they conquered, reclaimed, and colonized the pavement nightly.

They were, of course, flattened, out on the streets. There were no roads in the summer that were not decoupaged with the tarpaper-flat legacy of what and where they had been.

They were slippery and squishy beneath the wheels, at night, but the next day the summer sun quickly baked them paper thin. Mockingbirds and blue jays carried most of them away like miniature sandwich boards, but despite the nightly reduction, there were always more; they kept coming, again as if answering the tides.

My friends and I would some nights for entertainment walk up and down the sidewalks of our streets, collecting the living ones from beneath the streetlamps, simply to see how full we could fill our tall buckets. (There is nothing, I realize now, more repulsive than a boy.) The buckets grew heavy and stretched our arms, the toads hopped and wriggled and writhed, it was a strange sensation to be carrying the lives of so many in each bucket.

We would have wars with them. I don't mean that we used them as weapons, but instead, we set up rows and columns of tiny plastic green Army men at one end of our sandboxes, then emptied a bucket of a hundred or more toads into the other end of the sandbox, and watched, like Romans observing the Christians versus the lions, as the toads galloped over the tops of the Army men, the soldiers' rifles and grenades utterly ineffective against the power of the living. We would laugh to see how easily the infantry of mankind was crushed, laid to level beneath the advance of the legions of toads.

Firefly lanterns lined our bedside tables in the summer, back then. Cicadas whirred and crash-landed, spinning and buzzing at our feet, glittering jewels dropping like the bombs we practiced for in school fallout shelters but that never came. We stood in richness at the edge of loss—some would say at the edge of an abyss—and yet we did not see it. Our days were not freighted with foreknowledge. It was not so much an innocence as instead a blessing.

What blessings might we inhabit now, similarly unrecognized? They must be out there. They must be all around us, still.

RECORDS

IT'S CHRISTMAS EVE, and we're in Houston at my parents' house, and I'm watching *A Christmas Carol*, with all my grandparents home for the holidays. They're all ancient, and healthy as bulls: Grandma Robson, ninety-two and spry after breaking her hip a couple of months earlier—the first bone she ever broke—and my grandparents Bass, both eighty-eight.

I don't care how healthy you are, this human system of pipes and plumbing is only good for so far, and it's got to make a person nervous, when you get that close to the end, that close to lying down and going to sleep, to see ghosts—even if only on television—and coffins, and snow blowing across gravestones, and the terror in George C. Scott's eyes when he wipes the snow off one gravestone and sees his own name. And all the ghosts, all the dead, coming and going in that movie, and looking and sounding so unhappy and horrible—black robes, unmentionable faces, and above all, *so* unhappy. Everyone in the family figures, roughly, another decade for all of the grandparents: but then, no more. No way.

Those ghosts rattling their chains and shimmering in that blue ghostlight they have—half-here and half-not, and sounding so grisly: I was the only one in the room with the old folks—everyone else had gone to bed.

I'd like for the respect I have for all three of my old grandparents to come through between the lines, but to make sure it is understood, I'm going to go ahead and say it: it's there, and it's huge.

Each generation, I think, learns less and less about death these days, rather than more—and so there I am, in this room full of old people, my three oldest living relatives, and all of them in such wonderful shape.

I wonder how often they think about it.

Probably by this point they have got it all bucked out, and don't think about it nearly as much as one might suppose. Probably they made their peace with the aging of their bodies many years ago—these days, maybe it's all gravy; maybe they no longer fill their days with the push-ahead hurry to get things done, important things. Nor do they gaze upon sights, all sights, with both the terror and the wonder of things being seen for the last time— but rather, perhaps they simply go about their daily chores in a manner once again small and regular, like the rest of us.

But still: maybe it was just my imagination, but it seemed to me that this movie was making them a little nervous; that after a while, when it started to get really scary, my old grandparents, with everyone else gone, asleep with wine after the Christmas Eve dinner, were able to pull back and away from the movie's grip and its mood in a way that I was not.

"I just think it's a marvel that you're walking," Grandma Bass murmurs to Grandma Robson, turning her back on the television.

Grandma Robson starts to say something and then just shrugs, as if to say, the way she can with those shrugs, that everything's a miracle, but then, too, everything's the result of hard work. She rocks in her chair, remembering, I suppose, all the therapy sessions, and her having to train like a halfback.

Grandma Bass doesn't want to go back to watching the movie. I can see that she's feeling the keen chill of luck pass through her, a shiver that it had not been her, but that it could have been, and that it might yet be.

"So many of my friends break their hips, and that's it, they never walk again," Grandma Bass says, and Grandma Robson just shrugs again.

EARLIER THIS FALL, up in Montana, where I live now, I shot a deer. Killed a deer, hunted a deer, got a deer, took a deer off the planet.

I've been hunting all my life. I like to hunt, and I like the way I do it. I go off into the far woods by myself and do what I do, and when it's over, I carry the deer, or elk, out of the woods; I bring it home, process it, put it into the freezer. I won't defend hunting under the frail arguments of meat and population balance. I like doing it. I would not do it if I did not love venison, did not eat it—for that would be killing, instead of hunting—but still, I will not run for cover from anti-hunters beneath the argument of meat.

I like doing it. I feel sad when the big old deer is down, but still, I like, even love, to hunt.

Little bucks, generally, are easy to hunt. Usually they come to you, if you're quiet in the woods; or sometimes, you can walk up on them. Some hunters have a system of scoring points—measurements, based on the size of a deer's antlers—measurements that, frankly, sometimes bother me.

I love to try to hunt big-antlered deer—and this year, I got one—but I don't like this idea of measuring them, scoring them. I won't criticize the hunters who do this, because it's not my place to say they're wrong to love the pursuit of records, any more than it's someone else's place to say it's wrong for me to love to hunt—but still, I don't ever measure the big deer I shoot. I just hunt them, shoot them, and remember them.

Many of my friends detest hunting—I mean, close friends. They take active stands against it and even refuse to eat the game I've killed—grouse, elk, deer—when I fix it and serve it to them when they visit. They're not vegetarians—and they don't tell me I shouldn't hunt—they just boycott the food I have in my freezer.

I stay cool about it. I'm sorry for them—especially when I fix the grouse (with balsamic vinegar and figs)—and I think it's silly, but I'm not so dumb as to not realize that they think my hunting is silly, and they're biting their tongues, too. And who can say who's right, who's wrong?

Sometimes I feel like my friends are *frightened* of me—like there's this distance, between my soul and everyone else's. It seems like their lives in the city are so forward-moving, so ordered, so sure—and yet, for two months a year, hunting's almost all I want to do.

I want to get into those same woods that I hike in, in the springs and summers, only I want to *hunt* them in the fall. Everything's electric; the days matter.

When I'm hunting, I get lost. I love getting lost.

I WAS FORTUNATE enough to get a deer this year, up here in Montana, where one per year is the limit, by law: one deer and one elk. (I don't hunt the monstrous moose, which are slow and unafraid, which you can walk up on in the woods and touch with a feather duster, if you are brave enough. I did plink one once, with a slingshot I use on grouse, to try to make him wild, so he would run from record-hunters, if he heard them coming—but he only stared at me, and then snorted and, finally, charged. My heart flew up into my mouth, and I fell, running for a tree, but he was only bluffing, he turned and went back into the woods . . . .)

This deer I shot, this year—he's the largest I've ever seen. His antlers splayed everywhere, and his body was as big as a small elk's. I have no interest in or desire to swell myself up as a panther-of-the-woods, the way some record-hunters seem to do, because I know I'm not. There's skill, but there's also luck, and mostly perseverance.

The deer I got this year is—and I can tell, just by looking—some kind of monstrous record, but he was also a gift. It was grace that brought him to me.

I'd been out hunting all morning in a heavy snow and had seen two small bucks, deep in a jungle, but hadn't had a good shot on either of them: they were racing through the heavy trees. I'd come back home a little discouraged, and a little worried—because (this is not a defense) I *do* count on that meat. The steroid-meat in the stores scares me, consumed over a lifetime.

But this is not a defense.

I like to hunt.

My rifle was wet, so I stripped it and took the bullets out and oiled it and set it by the fireplace, and went in to eat breakfast.

My back was to the big breakfast room window. Elizabeth was drinking coffee with me, reading a magazine. We had a guest staying with us, and he'd just gone upstairs, thank goodness—he's not a hunter. Did he lure that deer to me? Perhaps.

"There's a deer in the backyard," Elizabeth said, rising, and even as I was standing myself, and turning, I asked, "Is it a buck?" There were two days left in the season.

I looked out the window and saw that it was not a buck, that it was a doe, and she was running hard across the backyard, and then came something I'd never seen before.

A huge buck came leaping out of the forest, sailing through the air—his antlers, and his violent, brush-crashing appearance so huge that he appeared *menacing*, as if, unbelievably, he had come to attack the house—and he was chasing that doe, running her. I ran over to the fireplace, grabbed the rifle, and ran out onto the back steps, knelt, and followed, in the scope, the rocking, stiff-backed run of this huge deer—following his neck and big-antlered head in my scope, the scope like a telescope, the instrument of death, a precision tool, bringing the deer and his huge antlers in to me.

He was racing about looking for that doe, intent only upon that doe, who had fled back into the forest—and then the buck paused, right before going back into the woods himself—one last frantic, wild-eyed, hard-dicked look of fierceness—where *was* that doe? The future was at stake!

I squeezed the trigger, his huge neck blocking the tiny crosshairs of my scope, and there was the click of metal, for my bullets were not in the rifle where they belonged, but were drying on a shelf—and the buck, though he did not hear the click!, lunged into the woods, to look for his heart's desire there, to look for what was running from him, what was *fleeing* him—and I cursed, meat lost, and ran back into the cabin and snatched up two bullets, though I did not believe I would ever see the buck again, and when I ran back out into the snow, he was gone.

I walked out through the snow to where the buck had been standing and looked off into the woods, up the mountain in the direction he had gone, and imagined how he was still running, how he might never stop running, and Elizabeth came out across the yard to the edge of the woods where I was standing, and we just stood there.

It was starting to snow, and I was wearing only my long underwear. My boots were still unlaced.

We stood there with the snow coming down, the snow landing on us, the snow burying the mistake—I'd spent all my life hunting, and hunting hard, but had never been presented with that kind of grace—and we both knew that we'd never see such a sight again.

"Well," Elizabeth said, finally. "I'm sorry."

"Boy," I said, or something like that. "He was big, wasn't he?"

"I don't guess he'll come back?" Elizabeth asked, and I laughed.

"I guess I'd better go look for him," I said. "I don't think I'll ever see him again, but I know I won't if I don't try."

I went back into the house, and dressed, and then went into the woods, with the rifle in one hand. The snow was coming down hard now, burying his big tracks quickly. I carried a pair of loose antlers in my other hand and wore a grunt tube around my neck. I walked through the woods, rattling those antlers from time to time so that it would sound like two bucks were fighting—banging their antlers against each other's—and I'd blow on the grunt tube, too, so that it would sound as if one of the deer was injured, or was angry, or was following a doe, calling to her.

I walked quietly and slowly for more than a mile. There's no surprise here. We already know that I did catch up with the deer; after a while, his tracks slowed to a walk, and then he began making circles, walking rings around trees to look back at the sound of the fight that he thought was going on behind him—a fight he must have been sure he could easily win.

Before I get to the part about how I saw him again, I want to put in a sort of postscript—about something I didn't know at the time, but found out later.

Some other people in the valley had been getting their deer from this same area—big deer—but they were complaining because a lot of those deer had puncture wounds in their rut-swollen necks—infected wounds that ruined the neck meat—where their big deer had been injured in fights with an even larger deer.

I never thought I'd see this big buck again. I was just following his tracks up the mountain, in that falling snow, more for penance than for anything else. I would follow his tracks for as long as I could pick them out from all the other deer's tracks in the woods, and until the falling snow filled them in. I would not get in a hurry. It was really just a sense of mild wonder with which I was following that huge deer—rattling those antlers occasionally, as if I really believed he was still out there, and grunting on the grunt tube, as if I were a deer myself.

I went into some heavy timber, the buck's tracks still making complete circles around trees and bushes sometimes, as he must have been pausing to look back.

When I came out of the timber, he was standing in a small opening, in deep snow, about fifteen yards in front of me, looking right at me—the sky a sea of antlers, all around him, like Medusa, and him standing in snow so deep that his great belly rested against the top of it.

I threw the rifle up—the scope was foggy from all the moisture, and I could barely see his outline through it, but at fifteen yards, one does not miss, and he lunged when I shot, hit in the heart, and ran across the tiny clearing and into more timber, where he fell dead, his big antlers tangling up in all the limbs and branches above him.

I cleaned him, and dragged him, with great effort—I could barely pull him—across the snow, and out to a logging road. Then I walked home to get the truck.

The dogs were happy to smell the blood on my hands and a spot of it on my pants, and I was pleased that I had gone after the deer, and found him again. Elizabeth was happy, both for me and the meat, and for the size of the deer, and also the proximity of it—usually I have to pack out several miles, making several trips, and it was starting to snow really hard.

I took the truck down to where I'd dragged him out to the road, and by crawling under the deer and lifting him with my back, I was able to roll him onto the tailgate and drive home with him.

The dogs went nearly berserk when I came up the driveway.

What is the moral? This is where I live now; this is what I do. Does there need to be a moral? We had meat for the winter. There had been three of us, in the valley—Elizabeth, and myself, and that big, missed, escaped deer, which would always have been lingering in my consciousness and later, my subconscious—but now there were only two of us again—and all that meat, and all those antlers, and all that snow coming down, late November, and only one day left in the season.

My life—it's moving along. I'm trying to sort out the things in it that matter.

GRANDMA ROBSON IS TELLING one more story, about how she fell off a ladder in her kitchen, when she was eighty.

This was eight years ago.

"I was putting dishes back up into the pantry," she says, "the way I always do—used to do, I mean. Putting them on the top shelf.

"I guess I got dizzy or something, and I just fell straight backwards." Grandma Robson's house is an old one, with high ceilings.

"I was way up that ladder," she says. "I just fell straight back, with my arms outstretched, and landed on my back, with my arms straight out like this"—Grandma Robson leans back and demonstrates the crucifix position—the movie forgotten—meaningless blue light in a box, electricity—we're listening to *stories*, now—Granddaddy Bass frowns and looks away, and Grandma Bass winces, almost afraid to listen—"and the floor shook when I hit, and dishes began to rain down all around me, sliding out of the pantry and breaking on the floor all around me. I wasn't hurt, miraculously, and all those dishes—plates, cups and saucers, salad bowls, china—just kept falling and breaking, and I was lying there on my back, looking up at the ceiling, and I got to thinking of how I must have looked, an old woman, and I had to just lie there and laugh."

RECORDS: I'M SURROUNDED by all this *life*, is what I'm saying, and some days it feels like I'm that deer, threading my way through the forest, this forest that's full of grace, and everything in it is safe, and yet everything is dangerous, too, and yet it doesn't matter, none of it. It feels like everything is heartless but full of grace at the same time—and I still don't know why I hunt, but it is enough to know that I enjoy doing it, and will continue doing it.

It's important not to overdramatize this. It's as natural, and as heroic—for the deer—as is growing old, or being hunted.

Being measured for records is meaningless—the oldest person, the biggest deer. Living and dying, and the in-between, is all that matters, and it's all here for the taking.

For me, I can't separate any discussion of hunting from a discussion of my family. We've always hunted—my father, uncle, brothers, and I. We gather our food. We gather the years. We are a family of hunters, even those of us like Grandma Bass and Grandma Robson, who do not hunt.

You wouldn't think one's eighty-eight-year-old grandmothers and deer hunting would have a lot in common—that they would be anything at all the same. But when I am out in the woods deer hunting, I find myself thinking about them a lot. The old ones. The things that have made us who and what we are.

THE OTHER FORT WORTH BASSES

FIRST OFF, HE SMOKES Viceroy cigarettes. They keep him skinny, like a bull-whip. He's almost eighty-eight and clear-eyed.

When Granddaddy was twenty-seven, he drove down from his home in Fort Worth into the Texas Hill Country, looking for some country to lease so he could deer hunt. He found the place he wanted by serendipity, or sixth sense, by just staying after it, wandering, looking, and all the while closing in on it. He found the place that would become his camp, and later my father's and uncle's camp, and my camp.

There are two creeks, which eventually flow into the Pedernales River. We regard water on the deer pasture as even more of a miracle than it usually is. In the Hill Country, the blaze heat bouncing off all those boulders and canyons makes us, as well as the wildlife, prize the water in those creeks.

Great live oak trees line the creeks, and scrub cedars blanket the steep hills. Shy deer and turkeys step through the dark cedars. Doves call. I've taken pictures along the creek of bobcats, foxes, coyotes, skunks, raccoons, quail, roadrunners, rattlesnakes. The deer pasture is a perfect mix of the rough (boulders, cacti) and the pastoral (small meadows, ponds, shaded creeks).

We chase that mix of nature every year in November, when all the men in the Bass family gather to hunt the first week of deer season. From wherever we're residing, it's a tradition that we can count on, one we look forward to all year: Granddaddy, my father and my two brothers, my uncle and *his* three sons.

Our family works mostly with the earth for a living, and always has. I'm a geologist, my father's a geophysicist, Uncle Jimmy threads and sells drilling pipe, and Randy and Russell, his two youngest sons, help him run the business.

Where once all the Bass men were bull *ruffians*, there's hope for Bass men to come. We're learning. There *is* hope. Uncle Jimmy's oldest son (also named Rick) is, of all things, a gynecologist. And his specialty is difficult pregnancies—fertility. He specializes in getting women pregnant, is how we refer to it.

I grapple with the earth, as a geologist, but I also write, and my middle brother, Frank, is a journalist. Not that writing is as feminine as gynecology, but it's still a far cry from shoving drilling pipe down into the earth. My youngest brother, B. J., manages our dad's ranch in South Texas, but plays tennis and the guitar.

There are two outcropping rock formations on the deer pasture, one of which represents some of the oldest known rocks in the world. Cambrian dikes and sills flowed through the land roughly one billion years ago. These granite formations were buried by the Cambrian seas, which left a thick deposit of iron-rich red sandstones, called the Hickory Sandstone. The younger granite is not as enduring or resistant as the iron-filled Hickory Sandstone. The old granite decomposes and releases its nutrient-filled minerals back into the soil. The pink feldspar in the granite decomposes into nuggets and gravels that we call chat, which is a beautiful pink-rose color. It's in the bottoms of all the creeks.

A hundred and fifty years ago, so say the old journals of the area, the Hill Country was almost all grassland. Then cattle moved in. Without steady wildfires, cedar swarms everything, though we try to keep it cut back. But it grows fast and tries to change the face of the land, tries to change things.

And we want to keep some meadows and grassland open, the way it was. Granddaddy, Uncle Jimmy, and Dad think it's silly that we boys work to keep the cedar out.

"Let it go," they say. "Just let it go."

But we want those soft green meadows: all that grass. We want to bring some of the meadows back.

There was a time, eight or so years ago, when Old Granddaddy was not so clear-eyed. He'd had a stroke at the age of eighty and we did not think he would make it another year. We thought that way for several years. Then he had surgery on the tendons in his wrists and hands, so that he could pull the trigger once more, and he learned to speak again. He got cornea implants that made his eyesight a perfect 20/20—better than any of ours. But he still smokes those cigarettes. He sits up in the granite boulders and, while hunting with the wind in his face, he inhales those damn Viceroys, which we won't let him into the lodge with because none of the rest of us smoke.

With the exception of Randy, who's a poet these days, and my father, who's becoming one, we're all hunters. Randy and my father prefer to watch the deer rather than hunt them. But Old Granddaddy is neither a hunter nor a poet. From the old school, he's simply a *shooter*. It's what he knows— shooting deer on this land—and it's all he's ever done.

There was a long dry spell, those years when we wondered if each year would be his last, when he didn't get a deer—when he couldn't even see a deer through the scope. Now it's like the old days. He shoots two deer a year (my father takes one home, and Randy takes the other) because that's the legal limit. It's also how Granddaddy is, and there's no need to try to change him, lecture, or judge him. If the limit were three deer a year instead of two, he'd shoot three. Not only do I not judge Granddaddy for being such an inveterate deerslayer, I am glad that he is. He gives our younger wanderings a dimension, a backdrop, and he gives us meat, too.

The severity of Granddaddy's sharp-eyed judgment, the harshness of sentence—the crack of his little rifle, a flat-shooting .222—contrasts nicely with the younger elements on the land. My brothers, Frank and B. J., or I will sometimes go off deep into the woods with a book in our coat pocket.

But our family's changing. The core of it's the same, but other parts of it, like the land, are changing, and it's a fine thing to see. Like in the evenings, when we sit around the fire and drink whiskey and talk about what each of us is doing, what has happened in the past year. We tell stories and listen, again and again, to the things that have happened to us in the past. We tell about the time that old Jack, the camp cook, picked up a pistol and shot a flying turkey.

We talk about *everything*. And in the old days—the way-back—we used to drink too much whiskey at night by the fire. We keep pulling back the past, pulling it back in as if it's attached to the end of a rope. Each year we sit around those campfires and strain to pull it all the way back in, like a bucket at the bottom of a well. Our intentions are to pull it in close enough to reach it, touch it, inspect it, *feel* it: to make sure it's all still in good shape and that none of it's missing.

My father's fifty-eight. I'm thirty-four. Soon it will be time for me to make my parents be grandparents.

My father tends to Granddaddy—Old Granddaddy. He pampers him, helps him hike all over the rough country, lifts and cleans and carries his kills in to the cabin we've built. He fixes Granddaddy's favorite meals—ham and biscuits with grits and red-eye gravy. Granddaddy eats these meals with a vengeance—leaning over the plate and shoveling the food in, eyes watering with the spice and pleasure of it.

Granddaddy usually crawls into his bunk around midnight. The rest of us stay out at the fire until two or so. Russell, my youngest cousin, goes through his usual phase of mixed melancholia-and-pride, sounding as if *he* is a grandfather. What he sometimes does is enumerate his company's successes until Randy, who's been looking east, looking out at the stars, looking out at Hudson Mountain, says, "Aww, Russ," or one of Granddaddy's old rallying cries: "Russell, you're the *shits*!"

It's just a phase, though, and we all know it. Russell will take a drink, look up at the night sky through the crazy sprawl of limbs above us, and he'll sigh. He'll be anchored, then, with Granddaddy and Uncle Jimmy and my father, Charlie, holding him down. Russell will stop talking of pipe sales, will stop speaking of Houston-town, and will no longer be the shits. He'll just be look-ing up at the stars. Then Randy will belch and say, "That's better, Russ."

It's all a cycle, and I have little interest in the short-term. I think it's the shits, too, when Russ starts talking about a single year. I want to talk about sixty-four years. And so do my uncle and father.

What Uncle Jimmy, who has a fierce, almost weepy pride in this clan of boys and men, does when he's in his cups at one or two in the morning and the thrill of all of us being together again consumes him, is talk about our family.

There are several Fort Worth Basses in Texas, and my grandfather had nothing to do with any of the other Basses. Granddaddy ran a country gas station on the outskirts of Fort Worth, out toward the village of Crowley, for forty years. Aside from the annual deer hunt, he took one vacation a year, to go fishing in Colorado each summer with my grandmother, a schoolteacher.

My father and uncle grew up poor—wash-clothes-in-the-bathtub poor, for a while. They married young, had children young—the web, the roots, beginning to spread—and then, after a long time, they were poor no longer.

My father and mother had a tough go of it at the beginning, too—before my father learned how to plumb the earth, how to reach deep. They hung the clothes out to dry in the West Texas wind.

My uncle, who has been spending too much time in Japan negotiating pipe deals, tells how the interpreters continue to ask him if he's one of those famous Fort Worth Basses. They're not talking about us, when they ask that.

My father, a geologist as well as a geophysicist, says he's been asked that question all over Texas, Louisiana, Mississippi, Alabama. Wherever he goes to find the oil and gas fields he's so good at discovering, they ask him.

He just says, "No." Perhaps he thinks about how it might have been if we were the wealthy Fort Worth Basses, instead of the other Fort Worth Basses, but I doubt it.

Pride can be a rough thing. It's not something easily eroded, nor is it eas-ily buried.

My father and uncle are asked this question wherever they go. And I'm sure that along with their reply is the memory of a dusty, lonely gas station on the outskirts of town. They say, "No, I'm not of 'the Fort Worth Basses,'" and then they recall sitting in the station drinking a pop, playing, while their father—Granddaddy—sits behind the counter, waiting for business.

We were raised outdoors, and it's been the blessing of our life. My father didn't have to raise me outdoors. He had worked hard enough and succeeded well enough to raise me and my brothers any way he wanted. He chose the outdoors just as Granddaddy chose this rough cedar country.

Our legacy, our blessing, has been to grow up on the land and to take from it while giving back to it, too. We learned to give the land our memories and love, to give it back respect, to give it back everything—including, in time, our bodies.

At the campfire last year, Uncle Jimmy talked to us about what it means to be a Bass. He went from son to son, nephew to nephew, and brother to brother, clasping his big hand on each of our shoulders—chewing his big cigar—as he talked to us not about the things a Bass does or doesn't do, but about the manner in which they're done. It has to do with being on the outside of the world rather than wrapped up in the center and noise of it.

Granddaddy's asleep in his bed by this time of night. But he's not far away; he's just inside the lodge. In his sleep, I like to think that he hears us: that some younger part of him hears what we're saying.

The stars flash and glimmer above us, the wind carries the smell of cedar. It's a cool night in the fall, and the fire is warm. The wind creaks the rafters of the big lodge behind us, the one we built by hand over the course of one summer. Our lives seem to have everything to do with rocks, with the earth: with things that last. Cool night air slides down off the top of the Burned-Off Hill and washes our faces. It's late. In the morning we'll go out into the woods again and move across the land.

My father taught me the boundaries and borders, the secrets of the deer pasture, and taught me how to hunt just as Granddaddy had taught him. Even now, I'm not remembering those old pictures of deer-gone-by, deer on the hoods of old jeeps, photos of past hunts before I was even born, but rather the sound my boots make when I'm climbing one of those sandstone ridges over on the back side and when I dislodge a pebble that rolls down into the canyon. I'm remembering the red rock canyons and the first time my father hiked with me back to Buck Hill and showed me the view.

This is one of the ways to write about my father: to write about the land he has chosen to keep walking across, and our place on it as a whole—the *net* of us, my family's men. If I had a choice—if I had to make one—I'd rather be in the woods than have money. I'd rather be happy than famous. If that were some kind of choice that ever needed to have been made, a long time ago, the men in my family decided to turn to the woods, rather than to the city, to spend more and more time in the woods, as much time as they could.

The view from the tops of these ridges at the deer pasture lets you see damn near everything. How far? Since it is the nature of a family of geologists to measure things in terms of years rather than miles, that horizon off to the east—where the flat top of Hudson Mountain looms—is seventy-five years distant, and changing every year, moving away from us all the time, even though we chase it.

I have to believe that we are gaining on it. It seems that we are.

ON WILLOW CREEK

I AM NOW ONLY THIRTY-FIVE YEARS OLD, and the land is more than a billion; how can I be expected to know what to say beyond "Please" and "Thank you"? The language of the Hill Country of Texas is not the language of pen on paper, or even of the human voice. It is the language of water cutting down through the country's humped chest of granite, cutting down to the heart and soul of the earth, to a thing that lies far below and beyond our memory. Being frail and human, however, memory is all we have to work with. I have to believe that somewhere out there is a point where my language—memory—will intersect with the Hill Country's language: the scent of cedar, the feel of morning mist, the blood of deer, glint of moon, shimmering heat, crackle of ice, scorpions, centipedes, rattlesnakes, cactus. The cool dark oaks and gold-leaved hickories along the creeks—the language of the Hill Country always seems to return to water. It is along the creeks where most of the wildlife is found.

The men in my family have always hunted deer—hunting them in Tennessee, and before that, in Mississippi, and perhaps all the way back to the dawn of man, the first hunter—perhaps the link across the generations is completely unbroken, one of the few unfragmented systems or notions remaining in this century—*The Basses hunt deer*—a small thing, but still whole and intact.

The land changes so much more slowly than we do. We race across it, gathering it all in—the scents, the sounds, the feel of that thousand acres. Granddaddy's gone now; Uncle Horace, John Dallas, an old family friend, and Howard, from whom we leased the deer pasture—already I've lived long enough to see men in my family live long enough to cross that intersection where they finally learn and embrace the real language of the earth—the language of granite, the language of history—leaving us behind, the survivors, still speaking in terms of memory.

We have not yet quite caught up with the billion-year-old land we love and that harbors us, but as we get older, we're beginning to learn a word or two, beginning to see (especially as we have children) how our lives start to cut knife-like down through all that granite, through all that ancient sandstone, cutting deeper and deeper into the stone hump of the Hill Country, until we are like rivers and creeks ourselves, and we reach the end and the bottom, and we understand.

WATER. THE CITIES AND TOWNS to the south and east of the Hill Country—Austin, San Antonio, Houston, LaGrange, Uvalde, Goliad—I could chart them all, thousands of them, for they are all my home—these towns, these cities, and these people drank from the heart of the Hill Country, the water in their bodies is water that has come from beneath the hills, the mystical two-hundred-mile-long underground river (it actually flows) called the Edwards Aquifer.

The water is gathered in the Hill Country by the forces of nature, percolates down through the hills and mountains, and flows south, underground, toward the ocean. Everything downstream from the Hill Country owes a thank-you to the Hill Country. The water that we don't drink or pump onto our crops or give to our livestock—that tiny part that eludes us—continues on to the Gulf Coast, into the bays and estuaries, where delicate moisture contents, delicate salinities, are maintained for the birds, the shrimp, and other coastal inhabitants that at first glance seem to be far away from and unrelated to the inland mountains.

A scientist will tell you that it's all connected—that if you live in Texas you must protect the honor and integrity of that country's core, for you are tied to it, it is as much a part of you as family—but if you are a child and given to daydreaming and wondering, I believe you'll understand this by instinct. You don't need proof that the water moving through those shady creeks up in the wild hills and mountains is the same that moves through your body. You can instead stand outside—even in the city, even in Houston—and look north with the wind in your face (or with a salt breeze at your back), and you can feel the tremble and shimmer of that magic underground river, the yearning and timelessness of it, just beneath your seven-year-old feet, and you can know of the allegiance you owe it, in a way that not even the scientists know. It is more like the way when you are in your mother's arms, or your grandmother's, that it's all tied together, and that someday you are going to understand it all.

When the men went north in the fall, I'd stand there on the porch with my mother and watch them drive off. It would often be raining, and I'd step out into the rain to feel it on my face—and I'd know that they were going to a place of wildness, a place where they came from. I did not seriously believe that I would ever be old enough to go in the fall myself.

Instead, I sought out the woods I could reach. We lived out near the west edge of Houston, near what is now the Beltway. We lived a few hundred yards from the slow curls of Buffalo Bayou. While the men in my family went up into the Hill Country (and at all other times of the year), I would spend my time in the tiny de facto wilderness between outlying subdivisions. Back in those still-undeveloped woods was a stagnating swamp, an old oxbow cut off from the rest of the bayou. You had to almost get lost to find it. I called it "Hidden Lake," and I would wade out into the swamp and seine for minnows, crawdads, mudpuppies, and tadpoles with a soup strainer. In those woods, not a mile from the Houston city limits, I saw turtles, bats, skunks, snakes, raccoons, deer, flying squirrels, rabbits, and armadillos. There were bamboo thickets, too, and the bayou itself, with giant alligator gars floating in patches of sunlit chocolate water, and hanging Spanish moss back in the old forest, and wild violets growing along the bayou's banks. A lot of wildness can exist in a small place, if it is the right kind of country.

This country was too rich to last. The thick oaks fell to the saw, as did the dense giant hickories, and the sun-towering, wind-silent pines. It's all concrete now; even the banks of the bayou have been channeled with cement. I remember my shock at finding the first survey stakes, out in the grasslands (where once there were buffalo) leading into those big woods along the bayou's rich edge. I remember asking my mother if the survey stakes meant someone was going to build a house out there—a cabin, perhaps. When told that a road was coming, I pulled the stakes up, but the road came anyway, and then the office buildings and the highway and the subdivisions.

THE MEN WOULD COME BACK from the woods after a week or so. They would have bounty with them—a deer strapped to the hood of the car, heavy with antlers (in those days people in the city did not have trucks), or a wild turkey. A pocket of blackjack acorns; a piece of granite. An old rusting wolf trap found while out walking; an arrowhead. A piece of iron ore, red as jewels. And always, they brought back stories: more stories, it seemed, than you could ever tell.

Sometimes my father or uncle would have something new about him—something that I had not seen when he'd left. A cut in the webbing of his hand, from where he'd been cleaning the deer. Or a light in his eyes, a kind of easiness. A smell of woodsmoke. These were men who had moved to the city and taken city jobs, who drove to work every morning wearing a suit, but when they came back from the Hill Country, there were the beginnings of beards. There was always something different about them.

AT THE MUSEUM OF Natural History every Saturday, I breathed window-fog against the aquarium panes, my face pressed against the glass as I watched the giant softshell turtles paddle slowly through their eerie green light. I bought a little rock sample of magnetite from the gift shop. The little placard that came with the magnetite said it was from Llano County, Texas. The deer pasture's thousand acres straddles Llano and Gillespie counties. This only fueled the fire of my love for a country I had not even seen—a country I could feel in my heart, however, and in my hands, to the tips of my fingers—and a country whose energy resonated all the way out into the plains, down into the flatlands.

All that sweet water, just beneath our feet. But only so much of it: not inexhaustible. We weren't supposed to take more than was given to us. That was one of the rules of the system. My father, and the other men who hunted it, understood about this system; for them, the land—like our family itself— was a continuum. Each year, each step hiked across those steep slickrock hills, gave them more stories, more knowledge.

I'd grip that rough glittering magnetite like a talisman, would put my fingers to it and try to feel how it was different from other rocks—would try to feel the pull, the affinity it had for things made of iron. I'd hold it up to my arms and try to feel if it stirred my blood, and I believed that I *could* feel it.

I'd fall asleep listening to the murmur of the baseball game on the radio, with the rock stuck magically to the iron frame of my bed. In the morning I would sometimes take the rock and place it up against my father's compass. I'd watch as the needle always followed the magnetite, and I felt my heart, and everything else inside me, swing with that needle.

When we run out of country, we will run out of stories. When we run out of stories, we will run out of sanity. We will not be able to depend on each other for anything—not for friendship or mercy, nor love or understanding. There are those who believe we should protect a wild core such as the Texas Hill Country because it is a system still intact, rife with the logic and sanity that these days eludes all too often our lives in the cities. I would agree, but think the Hill Country's core is worthy of protection too simply for its own sake, to show that we are still capable of understanding (and practicing) the concept of honor: loving a thing the way it is, and trying, for once, to not change it.

I like to think that in all the years we've been hunting and camping on that rough, hidden thousand acres—through which Willow Creek cuts, flows, forks, and twists, with murmuring waterfalls over one- and two-foot ledges, the water *sparkling*—I like to think that we have not changed it a bit.

I know that it has changed us. My grandfather hunted that country, as have his sons, and now we, my brothers and cousins hunt it with them, and already in the spring, we bring our young children into the country to show them the part, the huge part, that is not hunting (and yet which for us is all inseparable from the hunting): the fields of bluebonnets and crimson paintbrushes, the baby raccoons, the quail, the Zonetail hawks, and vultures circling over Hudson Mountain, the pink capital domes of granite rising all through the land, as if there once here lived a civilization even more ancient than their parents, grandparents, and great-grandparents . . .

A continuous thing is so rare, these days, when fragmentation seems, more than ever, to be the rule of the universe. I remember the first time I walked with my older daughter at the deer pasture. The granite chat crunched under her tiny tennis shoes and she gripped my finger tight to keep from falling. The sound of that gravel underfoot (the pink mountains being worn away, along with our bodies) was a sound I'd heard all my life at the deer pasture, but this time, this first time, with my daughter gripping my finger and looking down at the loose pink gravel that was making that sound, it affected me so strongly that I felt faint, felt so light that I thought I might take flight.

A country, a landscape, can be sacred in an infinite number of ways. The quartz boulders in my mother's garden—my father brought her one each year.

Other families had store-bought Doug fir or blue spruce trees for Christmas; we had the spindly strange mountain juniper from the deer pasture. Even though we lived to the south, we were still connected to the center of the state, and these rituals and traditions were important to us, so fiercely felt and believed in that one might even call them a form of worship. We were raised Protestants, but were cutting a very fine line, tightroping along the mystical edge of pantheism. When Granddaddy was dying, just this side of ninety, and we went to see him in the hospital room in Fort Worth, I took a handful of arrowhead chips from the deer pasture and put them under his bed. It seemed inconceivable to me that he not die as he had lived—always in some kind of contact with that wildness, the specificity of that thousand acres.

WHEN MY MOTHER WAS SICK—a small, young, and beautiful woman, all of her life—the strongest and best patient they'd ever seen, the doctors all said—she was ill for a long time, living for two years solely on the fire and passion within, long after the marrow had left her bones and the doctors could not bring it back, and still she never had anything other than a smile for each day she saw. When she was sick my father and brothers and I would take turns bringing her flowers from the deer pasture in the dead sullen heat of summer, the shimmering brightness. We'd ride around in the jeep, wearing straw hats. We'd get out and walk down the creek, down to the rock slide: stream-polished granite with a sheet of water trickling over it, a twenty-foot half-dome slide down into the plunger pool waiting below, cool clear water six feet deep, with a mud turtle (his face striped yellow, as if with war paint) and two big Midland softshell turtles (an endangered species) living in that pond. An osprey nest, huge branches and sticks, in the dead cottonwood at the pool's edge.

My brothers and I would slide down that half-dome, down into the pool, again and again. A hundred degrees, in the summer. We'd go up and down the algae-slicked rock slide like otters. We'd chase the turtles, would hold our breath and swim after them, paddling underwater in that lucid cold pool, while our parents sat up in the rocks above and watched. What a gift it is to see one's children happy and engaged in the world, and loving it.

We'd walk farther down the creek, then: a family. *Changed.* Fuller. My mother would finish her tea, would rattle the ice cubes in her plastic cup. She always drank her tea with a sprig of mint in it. At some point on one of our walks she must have tossed her ice cubes and mint sprig out because now there are two little mint fields along the creek: one by the camp house and one down at the water gap. I don't hunt there much any more: some, but not as much. I like to sit in the rocks above those mint patches for hours, and look, and listen, and smell, and think. I feel the sun dappling on my arms, and I watch the small birds flying around in the old oaks and cedars along the creek. Goshawks courting, in April. Turkeys gobbling. I like to sit there above the mint fields and feel my soul cutting down through that bedrock. It's happening fast.

SEEN FROM BELOW as it drifts high in the hot blue sky, a Zonetail hawk looks just like the vultures it floats with, save for its yellow legs. (Vultures' legs are gray.) The Zonetail's prey will glance up, study the vultures for a moment, and then resume nibbling grass. The Zonetail will drop from that flock of vultures like a bowling ball.

Afterward, if there is any left, perhaps the vultures can share in the kill.

Golden-cheeked warblers come up into this country from Mexico, endangered, exotic blazes of color who have chosen to grace the Hill Country with their nests in the spring, to place their hopes for the future deep in the cool shade of the old-growth cedars, the kind whose bark peels off in tatters and wisps, like feathers, and which the warblers must have to build their nests with.

As the old-growth cedar is cut to make way for more and more range land, the brown cowbird, a drab bully that follows the heavy ways of cattle, lays its eggs in the warblers' delicate nests, then flees, leaving the warbler mother with extra eggs to take care of. The cowbird nestlings are larger when they're born, and they out-clamor the beautiful gold-cheeked warbler babies for food and push them out of the nest. Why must the ways of man, and the things associated with man, be so clumsy? Can't we re-learn grace (and all the other things that follow from that) by studying the integrity of a system, one of the last systems, that's still intact? Why must we bring our cowbirds with us, everywhere we go? Must we break everything that is special to us or sacred—unknown, and holy—into halves, and then fourths, and then eighths, and then . . .

What happens to us when all the *whole* is gone—when there is no more whole? There will be only fragments of stories, fragments of culture. Even a child standing on the porch in Houston with the rain in his face can look north and know that it is all tied together, that we are the warblers, we are the Zonetails, we are the underground river: that some of it should not be allowed to disappear, as has so much, and so many of us, already.

Sycamores grow by running water; cottonwoods grow by still water. If we know the simple mysteries, then think of all the complex mysteries that lie just beneath us, buried in the bedrock: the bedrock we have been entrusted with protecting. How could we dare do anything other than protect and honor this last core, the land from which we came, the land that has marked us, and whose essence, whose mystery, contains our own essence and mystery? How can we *conceive* of severing that last connection? Surely all internal fire, all passion, would vanish from us in a second.

STORIES. ON MY UNCLE JIMMY'S left calf, there is a scar from where the wild pigs caught him one night. He and my father were coming back to camp after dark when he got in between a sow and boar and their piglets. The piglets squealed in fright, which ignited the rage of the sow and boar. My father went up one tree, and Uncle Jimmy up another, but the boar caught Jimmy with his tusk, cut the muscle clean to the bone. Back in camp, Granddaddy and his friend John Dallas and Howard and old Mr. Brooks (there for dominoes that night) heard all the yelling, as did their dogs. They came running with hounds and lanterns, globes of light swinging crazily through the woods. They stumbled into the middle of the pigs themselves. My father and Uncle Jimmy were up in the tops of small trees like raccoons. There were pigs everywhere, pigs and dogs fighting, men dropping lanterns and climbing trees . . . . That one boar could have held an entire *town* at bay. It ran all the dogs off and kept all the men treed there in the darkness for more than an hour, Uncle Jimmy's pant leg wet with blood, and fireflies blinking down on the creek below, and the boar's angry grunts, the sow's furious snuffling, and the frightened murmurs of the little pigs . . . . The logic of that system was inescapable: don't get between a sow and boar and their young.

The land, and our stories, have marked us.

MY FATHER AND I ARE GEOLOGISTS. Uncle Jimmy and his two youngest sons manufacture steel pipe and sell it for use in drilling down through bedrock in search of oil, gas, and water. Our hunting cabin is made of stone. We have a penchant for building stone walls. Our very lives are a metaphor for embracing the earth: for gripping boulders and lifting them to our chest and stacking them and building a life in and around the country's heart. I've sat in the boulders on the east side and watched a mother bobcat and her two kittens come down to the creek to drink. There used to be an occasional jaguar in this part of the world, traveling up from Mexico, but that was almost a hundred years ago. Granddaddy would be ninety this October. He and the old man we leased from, Howard, were born in the same year, 1903, which was the number we used for the lock combination on the last gate leading into the property. It's one of the last few places in the world whose system still makes sense to me. It is the place of my family, but it is more: it is a place that still has its own integrity, that still abides by its own rules. The creeks have not yet been channeled with concrete. There is still a wildness beating beneath the rocks.

Each year, we grow closer to the land, rather than farther away. Each year, it marks us deeper and deeper. The lightning strike that burned up the top of what is now called the Burned-Off Hill: we saw firsthand how for twenty years the wildlife preferred that area, but finally the protein content has been lowered again, and it is time for another fire.

The land and its stories, and our own, have marked us. The time Randy and I were picking up one of what would be the new cabin's four cornerstones to load into the truck. August; ninety-five degrees. Randy dropped his end of the behemoth sandstone slab (about the size of a coffin), but didn't get his hand free in time. It might have been my fault. The quarter-ton of rock smashed off the end of his left pinky finger. No more tea-sipping for Cousin Randy. He sat down, stunned in the heat, and stared at the crushed pulpy end of that little finger. Some small part of it was already ground and mashed in between the atoms of the rock, and a little blood already dripping into the iron-rich soil.

He tried to shake off the pain, tried to stand and resume work, but the second he did his eyes rolled heavenward and he turned ghost-white in the awful heat and fell to the ground, began rolling down the steep hill. All the little birds and other animals back in the cool shade of the oaks and cedars were resting, waiting for night to cool things off. What an odd creature man is. But we couldn't wait for night. We were aflame with a love for that wild land, and our long, rock-sure history on it. Our loving place on it.

GRANDDADDY KNEW THE OLD Texan's trick of luring an armadillo in close by tossing pebbles in the dry leaves. The armadillo, with its radar-dish ears, believes the sound is that of jumping insects and will follow the sound of your tossed pebbles right up to your feet before it understands the near-sighted image of your boot or tennis shoe and leaps straight up, sneezes, then flees in wild alarm.

THERE IS A STARTLING ASSEMBLAGE of what I think of as a "tender" life up there, for such a harsh, rocky, hot country. Cattails along the creeks, tucked in between those folds of granite, those narrow canyons with names like Fat Man's Misery and boulder-strewn cataclysms such as Hell's Half Acre. Bullfrogs, leopard frogs, mud turtles, pipits and wagtails, luna moths and viceroys, ferns and mosses . . .

The old rock, the beautiful outcrops, are the power of the Hill Country, but the secret, the mystery, is the water; that's what brings the rock to life.

It's so hard to write about such nearly undefinable abstractions as yearn-ing or mystery, or to convince someone who's not yet convinced about the necessity and holiness of wildness. It's hard in this day and age to convince people of just how tiny and short-lived we are. I remember one winter night, camped down at the deer pasture, when a rimy ice-fog had moved in, blan-keting all of the Hill Country. I was just a teenager. I had stepped outside for a moment, for the fresh cold air; everyone else was still in the cabin, playing dominoes. I couldn't see a thing in all that cold fog. There was just the sound of the creek running past camp, as it always has, and as I hope it always will.

Then I heard the sound of a goose honking—approaching from the north. There is no sound more beautiful, especially at night, and I stood there and listened as it drew close.

Another goose joined in—that wild, magnificent honking—and then still another. It seemed—standing there in the dark, with the cabin's light be-hind me (the *snap! snap! snap!* sound of Granddaddy the domino king play-ing his ivories against the linoleum table)—that I could barely, in that mo-ment, stand the hugeness, the unlimited possibility of life. I could feel my youth, could feel my heart beating, and it seemed those geese were coming straight for me, as if they too could feel that barely controlled wildness.

When they were directly above me, they began to fly in circles, more and more geese joining them. They came lower and lower, too, until I could hear the underlying readiness of those magnificent, resonant honks; I could hear their grunts, their intake of air before each wild honk.

My father came out to see what was going on.

"They must be lost," he said. "This fog must be all over the Hill Country. Our light may be the only one they can see for miles. They're probably looking for a place to land, to rest for the night, but can't find their way down through the fog."

The geese were still honking and flying in circles not a hundred feet over our heads. I'm sure they could hear the gurgle of the creek below, buried just beneath that fog bank. I stared intently up into the fog, expecting to see the first brave goose come slipping down through that fog, wings set in a glide of faith for the water, the harbor, it knew was just below, but which it could not see. *They were so close.*

But they did not come. They circled our camp lights all night, keeping us awake, trying, it seemed, to *pray* that fog away with their honking, their sweet music; and in the morning, both the fog and the geese were gone, and it seemed that some part of me was gone with them, some tame or civilized part, and they had left behind a boy, a young man, who was now thoroughly wild, and who thoroughly loved wild things. And I often still have the dream I had that night, that I was up with the geese, up in the cold night, peering down at the fuzzy glow of the cabin lights in the fog, that dim beacon of hope and mystery and safety and longing . . .

THE GEESE FLEW AWAY with much of my civility that night, but I realize now it was a theft, a welcome theft, that had begun much earlier in life. That's one of the greatest blessings of the Hill Country: it is a salve, a twentieth-century poultice to take away the crippling fever of too much civility, too much numbness.

All of the Hill Country's creatures had been helping me, in this regard, even before the geese came. It was along that same creek—Willow Creek—where as a child of nine or ten I had gone down to the creek with a flashlight to get a bucket of water. It was December then, too, Christmas Eve, and bitterly cold. In the creek's eddies there was half-an-inch of ice over the shallow pools. I had never seen ice before in the wild.

I shined my flashlight onto that ice. The creek made its trickling murmur, cutting down the center of the stream between the ice banks on either side, like a knife, but in the eddies the ice was thick enough to hold the weight of a fallen branch, or a small rock, a piece of iron ore.

There were fish swimming under that ice! Little green perch! The creek was only a few yards wide, but it had fish in it, living just beneath the ice!

Why weren't they dead? How could they live beneath the surface of ice, as if in another system, another universe? Wasn't it too cold for them?

The blaze of my flashlight stunned them into a hanging kind of paralysis; they hung as suspended as mobiles, unblinking. I tapped on the ice and they stirred a little, but still I could not get their full attention. They were listening to something else—to the gurgle of the creek, to the tilt of the planet, or the pull of the moon. I tapped on the ice again. Up at the cabin, someone called my name. I was getting cold and had to go in. Perhaps I left the first bit of my civility—my first grateful relinquishing of it—there under that strange ice, for the little green fish to carry downstream and return it to its proper place, the muck and moss beneath an old submerged log. I ran up to the cabin with the bucket of cold water, as fresh and alive as we can ever hope to be, having been graced with the sight and idea of something new, something wild, something—thank God—just beyond our reach.

FINALLY THE DAY CAME when I was old enough for my first trip up to the deer pasture. My father took me up there for "the second hunt," in late December. I would not go on a "real" hunt—the first hunt, the November hunt—until after I graduated from college.

My father and I drove through the night in his old green and white Ford—through country I'd never see, beneath stars I'd never seen. My father poured black coffee from an old thermos to stay awake as he drove. The trip took a long time in those days—more than six hours, with gravel clattering beneath the car for the last couple of hours.

I put my hand up against the car window. It was colder, up in the hills. The stars were brighter. When I couldn't stay awake any longer—overwhelmed by the senses—I climbed into the back seat and wrapped up in an old Hudson's Bay blanket and lay down on the seat and slept. The land's rough murmur and jostling beneath me—just under the floorboard—were a lullaby.

When I awoke, we had stopped for gas in Llano. We were the only car at the service station. We were surrounded by a pool of light. I could see the dark woods at the edge of the gravel parking lot, could smell the cedar. My father was talking to the gas station attendant. Before I was all the way awake, I grabbed a flashlight and got out and hurried out toward the woods. I went into the cedars, got down on my hands and knees, and with the flashlight began searching for the magnetite that I knew was all over the place. I picked up small red rocks and held them against the metal flashlight, to see if they'd stick.

When my father and the attendant came and got me out of the woods and asked where I had been going, and what I'd been doing, I told them, "Looking for magnetite."

We drove on: an improbable series of twists and turns, down washed-out canyons and up ridges, following thin caliche roads that shone ghostly white in the moonlight. I did not know then that I would come to learn every bend in those roads, every dip and rise. We clattered across a high-centered narrow cattle guard, and then another, and we were there.

It was so cold. We were on our land. We did not own it all, but it was ours because we loved it, belonged to it, and because we were engaged in its system. It dictated our movements, as surely as those of any winter-range deer herd, any migrating warbler. It was ours because we belonged to it.

We descended toward the creek, toward our cabin. The country came into view, brilliant in the headlights. Nighthawks flipped in the road before us, danced eerie, acrobatic flights that looked as if they were smothering the dust in the road with their soft wings. Their eyes were glittering red in the headlights. It was as if we had stumbled into a witches' coven, but I wasn't frightened. They weren't bad witches; they were just wild.

Giant jackrabbits, with their ears as tall again as they were, raced back and forth before us—leapt six feet into the air and reversed direction mid-leap, hit the ground running: a sea of jackrabbits before us, *flowing*, the high side of their seven-year cycle. A coyote darted into our headlights' beams, grabbed a jackrabbit, and raced away. One jackrabbit sailed over the hood of our car, coming so close to the windshield that I could see his wide, manic eyes, looking so human. A buck galloped across the road, ahead of us. It was an explosion of wildness, ahead of us. We had arrived at the wild place.

THE FIRST LONGING YEARS of my life that were spent exploring the small and doomed hemmed-in woods around Houston sometimes seem like days of the imagination, compared to the later days in the Hill Country. It seemed, when I went to Hidden Lake, or to the zoo, or the arboretum, or the museum, that I was only treading water.

I fell asleep each night with my aquariums bubbling, the post-game baseball show murmuring. That magic rock from Llano County, the magnetite, stuck to the side of my bed like a remora, or like a guardian, seeing me through the night, and perhaps filling me with a strange energy, a strange allegiance for a place I had not yet seen.

DEER CAMP

SOME YEARS WE NEED THE WOODSTOVE, other years the air conditioner. In the old days the season started in mid–November, around the peak of the rut, but for a long time now opening day has been moved back to the first Saturday in November. The lore from the old days is that of hunts amid ice storms and even flurries of snow: tales befitting those from a century ago. They used to sleep in wall tents, then a shabby old bunkhouse they threw together and shared with snakes and wrens and scorpions. Not until 1987 did we build a new and more hospitable bunkhouse.

The tin roof of it gets pounded by marbled hail, and, for those of us sleeping on the upper bunks, our faces grow chilled by each night's frost, and our hair stands on end during the electrical storms that cause the tin roof to crackle. On balmier nights the branches of overhanging oaks scrape and scratch against the roof like the soundtrack for an old horror movie. It's comforting, ancient, familiar.

Relatives of Davy Crockett had once owned this place, and before that, the Comanches. I like to think that the place was as special to them as it is to us, and from the incredible density of arrowheads scattered here and there—shards, points, spearheads, ax blades, awls—I believe it was. On one mesa I found ancient lichen-spattered sandstone rocks arranged in a perfect circle, the size of a teepee ring, with a view that looked over the entire Hill Country. Lower down, at the mouth of one of the canyons, there are fantastic granite monoliths, eroded into visages eerily reminiscent of the giant heads at Easter Island, and other boulders loom in the shapes of elephants, rhinos, clenched fists.

Every strong rain exposes a new sheet of shards and chips and still, all these years later, a perfect arrowhead. Now and again you encounter an old blue-tarnished bullet casing. The dozen or so of us who have hunted here every year have fired a lot of shells. If each of us shoots but once or twice a year, the math suggests there would be close to two thousand bullet casings breech-jacked into the brush, cartwheeling gold-glinting through the sun, to be lost for a while, until encountered by another, perhaps decades later, sitting in the same location, or passing through.

Some of us have shot more than once or twice a year. Over time, the deer tend to be drawn to the same shapes of the land—passing through the same slots and ravines and trails, often at the same crepuscular hours. By learning so well the shape of the land and the timing of the deer as they pass across it, we have found a curious way of slowing time down, or at least bending time, like a blacksmith forging an iron wagon wheel, into something less linear, something with an arc and, for all we know yet, ultimately a full circle.

The slow motion melt of our faces in the mirror, and our yearly photograph, picking up more and more lines in our faces: it's as if Granddaddy's coming back. It's as if we're all stepping forward. We're the same, yet we're different. Time is erasing the overburden of our destinies like the thunderstorms eroding the present to summon once more the past.

HOW CAN NATURE not develop in us a poetic sensibility? How can the specificity of the woods not spread through the canyons of our minds, bringing light and fuller understanding to all manner of broader truths, abstractions, similes, and metaphors?

As some of time's advancement reveals to each of us our previously concealed futures, our youth dissolving into the past that has preceded us, so too do we see pathways of disassembly being halted by time, held loosely together by a kind of time-in-balance. The beautiful pink granite with the fantastic cubic crystals of feldspar and mica (the larger and more developed the crystals, the slower the cooling) is going to eventually disassemble. The frozen fire cannot hold together forever, but for a little while longer, it appears that the rain-moistened lichens—brilliant turquoise, russet, blood red, and cornflower blue—are clutching the boulders so fiercely that they will never let them crumble.

The scientist in me understands that indeed there are processes in the lichen that, by extracting faint nutrition in the interchange between roots and stones, create a kind of acid that eventually decomposes the rock further. But the poet in me sees no acid, only the wildly intricate floral patterns of lichens growing broader each year and appearing to hold the boulders together.

In the morning after a storm the webs of garden spiders glint like necklaces in the spaces between the cedars, holding together the white spaces through which, soon, the world will begin moving once more, piercing the day, piercing the diamonds.

The more deeply we come to know this Hill Country place, the more we come to understand that there is a reassuring sameness everywhere. The green translucence of each sunfish in the little creek casts a delicate fish-shaped shadow when sun-struck, so much so that the shadow seems more real, more visible, than the fish themselves.

A hike through the high boulders on the east side of the lease—boots scritching on the pink wash of gravel that is the detritus of the decomposing granite—takes me past the tooth-shaped crystals of quartz that lie next to the bleached skull of a wild hog; teeth and savage tusks, loosened from his jaw, appear in their repose no different from the bed of ivory crystals in which he now rests.

Elsewhere on the same hike, far back in the brush, I encounter the skull of a bobcat, with its formidable rabbit-killing canines still intact, resting amidst a mound of dried rabbit pellets. Who controls whom, predator or prey?

I suppose we should be more intent upon finding and killing deer, but we have killed so many, across the decades, that it's not so much like there's a truce, nor is it a fatigue, as instead a desire, I think, for everything to move more slowly—to move as slowly as possible—and, as we all know, when you kill a deer, the hunt is over. At this stage of our lives, we are all less eager for the hunt to be over.

A close observation of nature cannot help but yield a poetic sensibility, and who observes nature more closely than a hunter? Not all hunters, however, devolve, or evolve, into poets. Certainly Old Granddaddy did not yield or change in this regard, but remained instead a resolute slayer of deer all the way to the end, chain-smoking cigarettes around the dry cedar all day. An eater of fried foods, particularly pork—"I never see a pig I don't tip my hat"—he probably would have lived to be about 120, had he had even remotely better habits. He's gone now, though steadfastly, we each and all follow him.

LIKE LITTLE ELSE IN THE WORLD, hunting demands presence and attentiveness, summons an imagination electric with possibility. Even as we age and lose the fire for killing and procuring—as if made weary by our relentless success—the habit of noticing nature continues. We watch how things in nature strive to hold together, even in the midst of massive disassembly, and we are comforted. We are comforted by the steadfast regularity of patterns—from the four seasons to the phases of the moon to the cycles of the deer in the fall breeding period, and everything in-between—even as our hunter's eye stays watchful always for the anomaly, the one interesting thing outside the cycle.

This ability to be two things in the world—pattern-viewer but anomaly-seeker—has sharpened who we are as a species and as a family and as individuals, and it occurs to me that stories serve the same purpose.

Each year we re-tell so many of the old ones—are reassured, re-knit together, by them—even as we seek new ones as well. Assembly, reassembly, disassembly: each year, we step through and between all of these stages. We keep moving forward.

Sometimes as we grow older we just want to sit around the fire and rest, but we keep moving forward, even knowing full well that it leads us right back to where we started.

WHERE ONCE COMANCHES raided the settlers who sought to eradicate their way of life, we now raid each other. Again and again we re-tell the old stories of gone-by pranks, while remaining vigilant for opportunities for new ones. Long ago, in his snake-fearing youth, a cousin who shall remain nameless killed a big rattlesnake—old-school Texas, back before people knew better—and he decided to bring it back to camp to skin and fry, curious as to whether it really did taste like chicken.

The snake was rendered headless before being tossed into the back of the truck and onto a pile of firewood that was being gathered for the campfire that evening. It was dark by the time he got back, and this nameless cousin straightaway asked his brother, Randy, for help unloading the vast scramble of limbs and branches.

Always an enthusiastic worker, Randy seized a big armful of wood, branches splaying every which-way, and as he was walking over to the fire, his face so close to the branches that he could barely see where he was going, I inquired, "Say, is that a rattlesnake in there with all that wood?"

Randy refocused upon the immense snake that was in the midst of his double-armful grip and threw the wood into the sky with a most satisfying scream.

Another time, I found myself walking back to camp alone, well after dark, without a flashlight. There was no need for one—we know every inch of the tangled thousand acres better, I think, than we know the canyons and corridors of our own minds—and walking in the darkness, still far from camp, I began to smell propane. I was walking along the creek beneath the high canopy of live oaks that formed a long eerie tunnel along the trail, and a short distance farther, I saw the spot of light that was the source of the scent: Randy with his hissing gas lantern. He's too old-school to use a flashlight; he likes the more democratic throw of the lantern for his night walking, and as I watched his lantern drifting through the all-else darkness like a firefly, a plan came to mind, one too good to pass up.

Knowing that he could hear nothing over the dull roar of the lantern, I ran down the dark corridor after him and drew right up behind him. Spanish moss hung in ghostly looping tendrils from the canopy. I took in as much air as I could and then let loose with the loudest panther scream I could muster, inches behind him, then jumped back out of the sphere of light as he dropped the lantern. The globe glass cracked and the mantles crumpled, but the twin burners kept jetting orange firelight.

Randy sat down promptly—in that tiny sphere of light, he looked pale and sick—and he peered wild-eyed into the darkness. "Richard?" he said, and I did not have the heart to scream again.

That was twenty years ago, and those days are gone now, all our hearts are too frail and worn-out for such shenanigans.

It's not just Randy who's the target of pranks; we all are. No one escapes. One year Russell shot a nice eight-point down in the creek. I heard his single shot, and knew he'd been successful. A few moments later, I saw a nice little forkhorn slipping through an opening on the other side of the creek, illuminated by the mid-morning sun on the side of Buck Hill.

It was a long shot but I had a good brace and was confident; I made the shot, and the buck dropped instantly. I climbed down out of the rocks, crossed the creek, ascended Buck Hill, cleaned the little buck, and then, feeling strong, began dragging him out, back toward camp, as had been done in the old days, rather than going to get a truck.

I had dragged it for only about fifteen minutes before coming through a clearing and seeing Russell's much larger buck, also gutted, hanging in a tree; Russell had already gone back to camp for a truck. His was a very nice buck, and I had no qualms about untying it from its limb, hiding it in the bushes, and replacing it with mine.

I then continued on to camp, where Russell was regaling everyone with the tale of his big deer. We were all excited to hear about it, and he was proud to show us, so after lunch we all drove out there in a caravan.

It pleases me to recall the confusion with which Russell slowly approached the deer—the disbelief in his face—and the way he turned to us slowly and said "*This is not my deer.*"

"Oh Russell," my father said, "they always look bigger when they're in the woods."

OTHER TIMES WE'RE LESS BRUTAL. As we age, we take midmorning naps more and more often, and our hearing is no longer keen. It's easy to sneak up on one another. We'll spy a hunter dozing against the trunk of a tree, camouflaged within the ground shrubbery of agarita or shin oak, and will slip right in and place a wildflower—a late-season aster—in the gun barrel, then pass on, unaccounted.

WE USED TO KILL DEER LIKE CRAZY. They were drawn to us as if by our desire alone. There were times known to each of us when we knew the day beforehand—the night beforehand—where we would see the deer. It was not with confidence that such certainty impressed itself upon us but instead a kind of wonder. The incandescence of our yearning for the hunter's con-tract—the way the world had lathed us, for at least the last 180,000 years—was at times a kind of brilliance within us, and we never took such dreams or foreknowledge for granted, but instead marveled at them, and the next day, moved toward those places—those appointments, those rendezvous—with the surety of faith.

And when the deer appeared, in much the time and manner as we had imagined, we were grateful, never arrogant. We understood that the success of such ventures never depended on our skill but was always instead the decision of some larger thing, some larger force—something a little like the electricity created by the confluence of our desire, the landscape, and the deer, as well as the world's desire to keep on moving.

To be hunters, we had to hunt—and to hunt, we had to be willing to gath-er our own meat. And back then, we were enthused about it.

Those kinds of dreams no longer occur. A central strand of the electri-cal current—our desire to find deer—has gone silent. Instead, now we sit quietly among the oaks and cedars. Sometimes the deer pass by us anyway, and sometimes—unless it is only my imagination—they almost look confused, as if wondering why their world has tipped, and where the hunters have gone. We admire the morning sunlight in their eyes.

We admire the smooth grace of their muscles. They have been here far longer than we have. They may or may not outlast us. Watching them pass by, it is very hard to imagine that any of it ever ends, but that instead it all goes on forever; that it, that current in which we once so enthusiastically participated, will last even longer than the stone itself.

THIS YEAR'S HUNT

THERE IS NOWHERE where we have not killed deer. The dimensions of our history on and love of this place are beginning to become significant, from either a deer's or a man's perspective, though not, I am sure, from a mountain's.

But it is an old story that time has a way of breaking things down (building other things just behind you, even as you are staring at the breaking-down), and eventually each of the hunters in our family dissolves the one mystery, topography (even while assembling new ones), and we learn each inch, each stone, of the deer pasture.

What are the cubic dimensions of a family's spirit? Nine men times seventy-six years times one week per year—days spent fully in the heightened sense of awareness that hunting brings—well, the cubic dimensions of things felt, land learned, senses touched accumulate to create within us, or impress upon us, like a stamp or a brand, something as new and deeply organic as a just-born, living thing.

It's like learning a foreign language. In the beginning, you seize upon a word or two, one whose shape or sound or translation has meaning for you. The great rounded granite boulder perched above the old camp on the lip of the bluff on the east side—visible almost from anywhere on the pasture. (I'll never know or understand why Old Granddaddy called it a pasture, *the deer pasture*, as if it were a damn croquet lawn or something, instead of hardscrabble rattlesnake and buck country.)

The flattop hulk of Hudson Mountain also in the east—shaped exactly like the lonely old buttes and mesas of our Hollywood cowboy movie youth.

The Water Gap, on the north end, where the big creek, Willow Creek, flows under the fence as it "leaves"—though it never leaves, the creek is still always there.

Turkey Hollow, once called Panther Hollow (my grandfather and sometimes even my father and his brother pronounced it "Holler," but my brothers and cousins cannot or will not, and so in that manner we are bending the language slightly, altering the story even more slightly, like rivulets of rain streaming down a mountain . . .).

You learn the outlines of the place—the fencelines, the roads, the rough shape—and then, over the years, you begin to explore the interiors, following the creeks and ridgelines at first—getting lost, finding yourself; getting lost, finding yourself—stumbling often. But then you begin to cherish getting lost—you seek out the deeper interiors, the really wild places—and out of that lost and groping stumbling, a fluency emerges.

They say that in learning a new language, one of the surest signs of fluency being achieved is when you begin to dream in that new language, and certainly, it is that way for us now, and has been for a long time.

There is nowhere on the pasture where we have not killed deer. They have always been there for the nine of us, now eight, across the years, and each year we kill a few, as if eating our way through the years on deer, or as if eating, gnawing at incessantly, the mountain, the thousand acres, itself; but the deer keep coming back, as if springing up out of the mountain, while it is we who fade and sink and erode and submerge, eventually, back beneath the surface.

Howard, the old man who owned the place so long ago, gone. Old Granddaddy, gone. And suddenly Uncle Jimmy's no spring chicken; nor is my father.

Hell, we're all getting old. Is it belaboring an obvious fact that when we first came to this place, we were young, and strong, strong as the rocks themselves?

And surely that is one of the finer or sharper ways in which we have each and all learned this landscape, have made our own interior maps of it. *If you follow this creek quietly up to its headwaters, you'll find the little mesquite flat where the ten-point was killed last year, grunted in shortly after dawn.*

This ledge is where you sat motionless for hours, a long time ago—you couldn't have been more than twenty-five—and where the eight-point emerged, material-ized, at dusk.

The stories, the micro-sites of where a deer fell, assemble like the patches of a quilt. You learn intently, deeply. You remember wind directions, soil type, pockets of dampness, species of underbrush. The land lives deeper in your mind after you walk away, whether you have killed or not—but I've found that the places where I've dropped a deer, then cleaned it and hung it, act in my mind as anchors or islands for the rest of the matrix.

Those places where the deer or turkey fell aren't necessarily more impor-tant to me than other places on the pasture. They just possess a depth, a res-onance, that seem more lasting, even unforgettable, in my memory. I pass by them, again and again, wandering, each year. Sometimes I will kill a deer not ten or twenty yards away from where I killed one in earlier years. I'm sure that when such analytical tools are available, it will be figured out that such happenings consisted of a perfectly equal mix of chance and destiny. It's re-ally not even worth worrying over or grappling with. That's just how it goes: a forced move in a designed space with "closed" borders—only a thousand acres, but a lifetime, several lifetimes.

The senses are inflamed and connected during the hunt; after the kill, in the stillness, as you sit there for a moment with the thing you have taken, the thing you have been given, the world seems truly frozen in time; and it remains stopped as you begin to clean the deer.

After a little while the world (glittering in its beauty, and you, amazed at your luck) begins to move again, though so slowly—and you become aware for the first time, though only dimly, as you drag or tote the deer (gripping him by the mahogany antlers), that had you not killed the deer, he might be across the creek by this time, further into the day, browsing oak leaves or nibbling at grapevine. But that is not how it turned out, and you continue hauling the deer, dragging it out to a road so that you can drive it back to camp and hang it from the bar from which all the years' previous deer have hung, to age in the night breezes and day shadows for a day or two before being rendered by your hands and the steel blade: backstrap, rib skirt, tenderloin, neck loin, neck roast, shoulder, ham, butt steak. Ribs like a bird's ribs. You know the workings of a deer's muscles, a deer's body, as well as your own.

All afternoon, the world moves for you at that slower pace. Maybe biology can explain it all by "causing" that lovely, wondrous feeling of completion to be a desired state for the hunter-gatherer so as to give positive reinforcement for replication in all the years or hunts to come. Whatever it is, and whatever its reason, it's strong and strange, and the shape of it fits a space in me, as I bend and flex to learn the shape of this land, those thousand acres, draping myself across it.

THIS YEAR, MIDWAY UP the backside of the Burned-Off Hill, moving through the cedars, I spooked two does, who bounded away. A buck was following them, walking as if drunk on their scent, and I fired, but missed; when I went over to look for hair or blood, to be sure I had indeed missed, I found the branch the bullet had hit, sparing that deer's life for a bit longer.

I looked long and hard anyway, to be sure. In the end all I found was an ancient gray cartridge, a spent 25.20, which is the caliber my father and uncle used to hunt with when they were young, more than fifty years ago. There was just the one cartridge, indicating in all likelihood that they'd made a kill. (My grandfather used to listen to the shots in the distant hills and count the number of times a hunter fired, telling us, "One shot, good shot, two shots, maybe, three shots, bullshit," the principle being, back then, when you could see farther—before the cedar crept in all over the hills like Einstein's wild hair—that if you shot only once, it meant you'd dropped the buck.

The second shot, following the miss, might be a hit. Sometimes the buck would be so surprised by the noise that he would pause, not wanting to run until he could figure out where the shot came from—*maybe*—but by the time a hunter had fired a third shot, if he did, that buck would most surely be up and running, wide-open, and if the hunter had missed the one or two standing shots, there was no way he was going to connect on a running third. *Bullshit.*

Now, however, the cedar has clotted almost all of the spaces between the oaks, so that the land, despite its aridity, is a jungle, a miasma of interlocked limb-and-branch. You see the deer but once, a wraith, as you yourself must be a wraith, trying to move through that clotted jungle, or sitting very still, waiting for the all-but-silent approach of the deer. One shot is all you get now, hit or miss.

THE REASON, OR THE MAIN REASON, the hills are becoming overrun with cedar—or so it seems to us, who first learned the land when there was not so much cedar—is that our white culture, ever since we arrived here in force, has been putting out fires of any size or shape. Fire is the enemy of cedar, which has thin bark, and cannot withstand the fire's heat. The oak trees, which bear the mast so favored by deer and turkeys, has a thick, "corky" bark and does well with fire, traditionally surviving the frequent low-intensity fires that once washed across this land like summer rainstorms, keeping the cedar at bay.

Now, in the long absence of fire, the encroachment of the cedar has become like its own kind of fire, spreading rapidly and at wind's whim: crawling, leaping, climbing, growing. It is not a new story or lesson—that in attempting overmuch to hold a thing back, you nurture the forces required to release it—but it is new to us, and sometimes now it seems that I can hear the crackling of the cedar as it grows from one year to the next, ever taller and thicker, obscuring—as if already to ash—the places where I walked and hunted as a child, and then a young man.

OTHER BORDERS, boundaries, relationships, are shifting, too. Uncle Jimmy had a stroke at his home in Houston, a big stroke, and spent the year recovering the use of his right arm (not to worry, he's a left-handed shooter), as well as the mysteries of speech. He still goes into work for a few hours every day, but the only words he can really master at present are "yes" and "no."

It made a graceful kind of sense—not overly pleasant, but acceptable, in a rough way—to watch Old Granddaddy get old, near the end; to care for him, on those last hunts of his, driving him out to an easy crossing where deer were likely to be active, and setting him up, and tending to him. (Some of those years, even after *his* stroke—including his eighty-seventh year, his last—he would get a deer, bracing the little .222, the lightweight flat-shooting gun in the crook of his elbow, and with his unblinking eye made briefly young again through the scope's optics, squeezing the trigger once more, and the deer would leap, then fall.)

He and Howard were the ones who taught Uncle Jimmy and my father, Charlie, how to hunt; and then there at the end, my father and Jimmy helped Old Granddaddy to keep hunting. It made full-circle sense.

But now, already, to see the men who taught my cousins and me how to hunt becoming so much older—to see my father, five years younger, assisting Uncle Jimmy, buttoning his sleeve for him, or tying a boot lace—I'm not ready for it. I'd like time—long time, not just the short time that transpires in the hours and days after you've killed a deer—to slow down a little. But it won't.

You would think that dealing more directly with death, as a hunter does—acknowledging actively that we live at the expense of the space and sometimes lives of others—that it would be easy to watch one's elders fade away, settling slowly back down into their beloved land, near the end of full and intensely lived lives.

But it really doesn't work that way. You might be one or two steps closer to accepting it—that place in the cycle. But here is still a gap in the witnessing of and participation in the unraveling of a family and a time. Only the place remains.

When I speak of the hunting of deer, I don't mean at all to be wading toward an attempt to defend that way of life. Better men than I have tried to explain it and, in my opinion, have come up wanting. (The older I get, such an effort—*defense*—seems more and more like trying to defend the sky, or the weather.)

I'm only trying to explain how I came to learn a landscape.

THE MOUNTAINS ARE CRUMBLING before our eyes. It's an amazing privilege, to see this speeded-up view of the geologic process framed and compressed within the blink of a human lifetime. Not all of the mountains are crumbling; some, like the Burned-Off Hill (which last burned in 1907), are composed of some of the oldest exposed rock in the world, the early Cambrian sandstones. They've been here for more than a billion years and will probably be around a little longer. The earth's yawnings and stretchings have fractured them in places along the lines of their initial calm-water deposition, square to rectangular, so that they are perfect for building stone walls.

I would go so far as to say they are alluring in this regard; that the beauty of their shape gives rise to the *idea* of a stone wall, and for many years in my spare time I have been playing with these exquisite stones, making walkways around the cabin, and low stone walls. I like particularly the leaden density of these flat and square rocks—the enduring stoutness of them—and I like too the peculiar odor that arises from them when I accidentally drop one against another. A sift of dust-powder will arise from the point of fracture, and I'll smell an odor that's been trapped in that hundred-pound stone for ten thousand millennia.

But the land here is no one thing; the eastern boundary of it possesses one of the rarer geologic events in the state, a system of exposed granitic batholiths: places where the earth's guts roiled in her fire-belly, seeking and searching their way along seams of fracture of weakness in the stony earth far below—boiling, following those underground cracks and crevices like, I imagine, a hunter—wolf, lion, cat, coyote—following indefatigably the track or scent of some quarry.

The fire-guts were stalled, at some point, never reaching the surface, where they finally gave up the hunt and cooled, very slowly; and as the magma cooled, the elemental minerals within began to settle, establishing certain and careful geometric arrangements that they had heretofore been unable to assume, dominated as they were earlier by the relentless force of the magma's search for the surface.

The magma, trapped beneath some ancient lid, cooled very slowly. The minerals—plagioclase, feldspar, zinc, silica—had all the time in the world. They floated, drifted, and spun around one another, according to ionic differentials, attractions and repulsions, as if in a waltz to some distant tinkling subterranean (or perhaps celestial) melody.

They stacked and ordered themselves into crystalline palaces that would have glittered beyond the imagination, had any light been present to reflect upon them.

There was, of course, none: only intense, total darkness, and a heat, a fire, cooling through the centuries.

Up above—and how far above? Five hundred feet? A thousand? Five thousand? We have no way of knowing, will never know, it has all been swept away and redistributed to the sea and the wind—the world continued gnawing, in its achingly slow and steady fashion, at the breastplate of stone, the lid, covering these gigantic palace domes that were being built below. Rain, frost, fire, wind, *time*. Rain, frost, fire, wind, *time*.

And slowly, so slowly—like the head of some colossus, some gargantuan thing emerging from beneath the waves—the tops of the buried palace domes crested, breached, the rubble overlying them in that manner.

That which they had not been able to reach all the way on their own—the surface—was brought down eventually some distance to accommodate them. As if the earth truly desired that beauty to be exposed. It would have taken millions of years, perhaps hundreds of millions, for the steady forces of the world, working without thumbs and fingers—no pry bars or other tools—to carve away that dense overburden.

And now, only now, the pink glittering world of granite, friable and delicate, exposed fully, resting frozen on the shoal of the old bank, the fissure-line along which it once surged.

The granite—rearranged now as it is mostly into wads and chunks of crystal—isn't long for the world. It's as if that's always been one of the laws of the world: a thing can invest itself in style or substance, but that to do so overmuch in one area often comes at the expense of the other.

So it is with the beautiful crystalline pink domes and pyramids and svelte hourglasses of granite that crowd the east side as if set there like giant play-toys or modern art. Without the stony overburden to protect them, and consisting of more crystal than matrix, the giant shapes are crumbling. The pink clay-rich minerals that held them together—plagioclase and orthoclase feldspars, mostly—are dissolving like sugar beneath the force of the real world; no longer supple with the life of their underground fire, they crumble and are carried in streams and runnels across the hills, as are the fantastic crystals the matrix once supported.

The boulders will still be here, strange and round and weather-sculpted into the shapes of the heads of elephants and men, long after we are gone. But they are diminishing so fast that each year it's possible to find a new trail of crystals leading away from one of the monoliths. It's possible to watch smaller chunks—those the size of a fist, or even a human head, perched out in the open, unprotected—vanish completely over the course of only two or three decades, leaving behind only a loose pile of pink and black and gold crystals, and then, following another decade of wind and rain, nothing.

The creeks glitter with the talus of these abrupt leavings. Sometimes when a crawfish scuttles across the pink graveled bottom of a clearwater creek, or a frog plunges deep to escape your approach, their impetus stirs the finer, flatter flakes of pyrite, so that left in these small creatures' wake is a vaporous, sifting trail of fine-ground gold, shining and glittering in aqueous columns of green sunlight, like wisps of smoke.

THERE ARE LEAVINGS of another kind, too, scattered across the hills and mountains here. Along the western fenceline, on the backside, back in the rugged red ridges of sandstone country, in one certain gully, lie the scattered fossilized leavings of what seems to me to surely be fossilized deer antlers. They are the precise shape and symmetry of the antlers of today's deer, though slightly smaller.

This might indicate a smaller-bodied animal, which might suggest a larger population, and/or a warmer climate, since a smaller mammal is more effective at shedding body heat, per unit of surface area, than is a larger one. Rest assured, though, that if the climate here was once warmer, it would also have been at another time cooler. Charles Darwin could just as easily have been speaking of climates and vegetative patterns when he wrote, "Daily it is forced home on the mind of the geologist, that nothing, not even the wind that blows, is so unstable as the level of the crust of the earth."

These stone antlers rest now atop the bone-white sheets and folds of caliche, a clayey mixture of weathering limestone that is itself the remnant, the skeleton, of where a shallow sea once lay—the same sea that has retreated now two hundred miles southward, but that will, when the world warms further, come rising, creeping, swelling back in, like tongues of flames, lapping and flickering.

Other leavings, in some ways less ancient, yet in others, more: the chips and flakes of Paleolithic men and women, fractures of arrowheads, stone knives, spear points.

The best time to find the flint and chert arrowheads is following a heavy rain, when the running water will have sifted away some of the chat to reveal new arrowheads buried years earlier. How strange it is to think of the arrowheads, stone echoes from the work of men's hands, rising and falling in this manner like the notes of music, or, more crudely, like the lift-and-fall synchrony of piston-and-valve—restless burial, emergence; burial, emergence.

My mother, who did not hunt deer but who nonetheless enjoyed this land, used to be far and away the best at finding the arrowheads. I've found a few, but nothing like her finds. She rarely went out for a walk without coming back with one. It wasn't so much that I was watching the forest for deer or the sky for birds and the direction of the wind, while she kept her eyes on the ground, for I studied the ground too, searching for the tracks and leavings of things. It was more that she knew what she was looking for, to the exclusion of all else. Again, it is one of our oldest lessons, that you can look right at a thing without seeing it.

The way things repeat themselves, across time—not just in the replications and recombinations of family and place ("He favors his momma, she favors her daddy"), but in the accretion of like patterns—as if somewhere far below (or high above), there is one and only one rule—though heaven knows what that rule might be.

A geologist sees it in the shapes and folds of the land; dust blown or washed away tends to be laid upon other parts of the land somewhat as a blanket is laid over the body of a person in a bed, retaining and perpetuating the sleeping shape below. But you can see it in other forms, too, on any walk in the woods. Searching for arrowheads in the fresh-washed streamside chat on the morning after a night thunderstorm, you'll bend down to pick up what you're certain is an arrowhead—a dark one, perfectly shaped, with concoidal flutings and rib-ridges reflecting the morning sunlight with a wet glint—only to realize, at the last moment—the moment of touch—that it is a small dried brown oak leaf.

What joke, or grace or beauty, of the world called for the weapon that hunted the birds—the little stone arrowheads that were called "bird points"—to be shaped exactly like the foliage in which the birds hid? As if always, in the shape of our protection and nourishment lies also the shape of our undoing. Hints that the world is either far more vast, or infinitely smaller, than we have previously considered.

I REMEMBER ONE morning at deer camp when my grandfather took me up into the round granite boulders above the old camp to show me what he said was a cache of "Indian jewelry." Central to that astounding, massive stonework, so suggestive of a civilization that had lived before ours (and, truth be told, suggestive too, by both the scale and beauty of the stone shapes, of a civilization somehow more grand and noble), is a broad vein of quartz pegmatite—a mysterious zone within the granite where pure silica—sand— settled in the cooling, once-fiery suspicion and then grew, as if in some garden, quartz crystals of the most amazing size and delicate complexion.

That line of white quartz hardened, then, like some salty artery, and the granite covering that encased it began to disintegrate. And in its decomposition, the granite released those quartz boulders, cobbles, and nuggets, which did not disintegrate, but instead lay stranded more or less where they fell, stranded now by the ghosts of the gone-away granite that once housed them.

There is one place on the pasture, above all others, that is flooded with these specimens; the forest floor is *coated* with nothing but beautiful shards of brilliant quartz, whiter than snow.

My grandfather was born in 1903, not yet a full generation removed from the time when the last of the Comanches and other tribes had been killed from the state. As a young man I remember being amused by the way, or so it seemed to me, he was suggesting that the Indians, bless their savage hearts, didn't know any better: that, lacking the superlative accouterments of our present culture, the quartz was all they'd had to make do with. As if these exquisite shards of quartz were less amazing than "true" diamonds, jade, and opal. Like children who didn't know any better, assigning outlandish value to things clearly of no value.

(I was a young man, in my early twenties, when he took me up there to show me the place of the Indian jewelry—which I had seen in my wanderings before, but had never considered to be the leavings of humans, but rather, the traces of some faraway geologic event: cold, beautiful, but impersonal. What interested me as much about my grandfather's revelation was not so much the subtle satire he seemed to be aiming at the Indians, for believing quartz was a kind of jewelry, but rather the way he explained and showed the place to me—The Secret Treasure House of Indian Jewelry. I think in his mind then I was still a teenager, or even younger, and that I would have a child's interest in such stories; that I was frozen in his mind from some earlier time—the age of ten or twelve, perhaps—as he is now frozen in time in my mind.)

At the time, I disbelieved him, though I did not argue; what harm was there in an old man's vision of naked red men gathering and exclaiming over crude crystals, which would never be seen by a jeweler's appraising eye?

Only recently have I begun to believe my grandfather's story and have likewise pictured the residents of a place picking up any quartz crystal they found in the area and bringing it—for whatever reasons: homage, respect, tithing—to this one central place, beneath and within the overarching granite monoliths, not far from the creek's edge, where surely they would have camped, as we do now.

Why else would all the quartz pieces be gathered in one place? Surely so rich a pegmatite would not have been confined to one spot, not much larger than a backyard garden. I believe they *were* worshipped, or at least celebrated (as my mother and I celebrated the arrowheads we'd find, or crystals, or stones, by placing them on the table or windowsill of camp).

Certainly, whatever positions in which they were arranged back then, if any, have been restructured by time's passage—by the effluvia of a thousand, or ten thousand, rainstorms, with quick bursts of runoff tumbling the smaller quartz pieces like rolled dice down the slopes of the granite mountain, so that in their altered and changing arrangements it is as if you are viewing the cursive script of some sentence still being written.

(In the milder oak flatland just above the creek, and above the civilization of granite, the animals often spend their winters—deer, wild pigs, bobcats, coyotes—and it is there on the shelf-land above that you will often find the loosened bones from the skeletons of the animals that did not survive the winter, with the sun-brightened curls of ribs and the spurs of vertebrae and the bowls of skulls disintegrating their brief hold on order, form, and integrity, and sliding downward, white as quartz, in sentences very similar to those of the stones' marking . . .)

A thing I've noticed we'll often do, as my cousins and father and uncle and I wander these thousand acres, is to pick up certain fragments of arrowhead or crystal or bone or antler pleasing to the eye, when we happen across them randomly in the field, and place them, as if on display—or again, as if in celebration, and admiration—atop some larger, more permanent stone.

Down along the creek, particularly in the area of the Indian jewelry, where it is damp and shady, rich velvet green moss grows on some of these rough boulders, though it can find no purchase on the slab-smooth crystal faces of the quartz. In particularly wet years, the moss flourishes verdant, and the luxuriant growth of it—an inch or two thick, and again, soft as velvet forest green-colored—lifts the single gleaming, tiny crystal, rain-washed and brilliant, placed there aloft on that bed of moss, atop that great table of a stone, so that it looks for all the world like the one specimen, the one gemstone, most desired of any jewelry, and on a display made more beautiful by the exclusion of any others.

ALMOST ANYWHERE ON THE deer pasture, one can come across seemingly improbable structures, so curious in their isolation out here in the backcountry. Lattices of dry cedar, cairns, stone walls . . . . Some I know were built by my ancestors (including the strangely Gothic pig traps, wire corrals that were built far back in the woods in an attempt to lure in and then capture the sometimes savage giant wild hogs that would occasionally terrorize the hunters at night; the corrals, the traps, are now enmeshed with vine and brush, and forty- and fifty-year-old trees are growing within the cages now, as if captured).

Other structures I do not know. The mysterious, wandering stone wall at the south end of the property is perhaps the most baffling. The stones that have been stacked there hint vaguely of the ceremonial, of the amphitheater—they face the magnificent hill of gleaming round granite boulders—but beyond what our impulses tell us, we have no clue; no record exists.

The work is somehow reminiscent of Europe, of white men's work. I don't mean this in a negative way, unless it is negative to whites—the near-lunatic mindlessness of stacking rocks—only that it seems, well, extravagant. By all accounts, there was not an overabundance of leisure time for the native peoples living here before us, and I've never heard of any stone wall builders in this region: only hunters, moving around here and there, following game.

My father is of the opinion that it was a corral for the Comanches' horses, but I'm not so sure: the wall is only knee-high. Even if it had once been chest-high, but the upper half had fallen over, you'd still see the scattered flat rocks at the fence's base, especially after only such a short time ago—a hundred and fifty years.

I don't think the wall was ever much higher than it is now.

We've never been able to find any artifacts: no rusting cans or nails, detritus of the white man era, nor any artifacts of stone, from the time before.

But the rocks are definitely human-stacked, and the effort involved implies a large number of people, as does the area bounded by the knee-wall: about five acres.

It's possible to imagine a long-ago time of druids, a forgotten or never-known time to us—a mysterious time, washed away and vanished, never-seen. The size of the stones in the wall are larger than those of any other rock wall I've ever seen. I wouldn't guess that a dozen strong men could have even budged any one of those huge square stones, much less hauled them whatever distance and fitted them into place.

And yet, they are fitted; they are erratic enough, stacked and platy enough in places, to erase any ideas that perhaps the earth just weathered in this location to erode and reveal the shape of a rock wall. It was definitely put here by someone before us, and my hunch, my gut, tells me that it was someone long before us, far before even the idea of us.

THIS YEAR MY YOUNGEST cousin Russell shot a small buck on the back side of Buck Hill an hour or so after sunrise; he had been walking, then sat down for a while, and the buck came walking past, feeding. Any hunter knows that there are cycles in the woods that tell you, and the other animals, when to get up and walk, and when to lie down and be quiet for a while—you can feel these waves or cycles moving in gentle pulses—and often I like to just sit there and be made slowly aware of them, in a way that I usually have not felt since the last hunting season.

The transition is often preceded by a long stillness. Something will shift, then—something silent and invisible, but as real as the mechanics of a cog—and you'll feel something, *the world*, lift; you won't be imagining it because a moment later, birds will begin singing and fluttering, and you'll suddenly feel an increased focus, and a slowing of your heart, a pounding. Your hearing will become sharper—the animals are moving—and sometimes, a few moments later, a deer will step into view, and perhaps it will be your deer, the one you intend to take that year.

I heard the shot—one shot—and knew where it came from, knew who it was.

That evening, with not fifteen minutes of light left, my middle brother, Frank, shot a spike on the east side. (I'd spent the morning not far from there with my youngest brother, B. J., rattling antlers and giving deer calls, trying to lure a deer in for him, but with no luck.)

Frank left his deer for me to clean and take back to Montana—he's a journalist in New York and has a very small freezer—and B. J. went back to school the next day.

The day after that, walking quietly on a sunny morning after the fog had lifted, I happened upon a big spike who was browsing cedar. He had his neck outstretched like a giraffe—does the cedar at canopy level taste better than that below?—and the branch shaking was what caught my eye. He had long antlers and I could see the tips of them shining in the sunlight. I was very close to him but he couldn't see me because the cedar bough was over his face like a mask, and when I shot, he crumpled without another movement.

I cleaned him, dragged him out to the road, then went and got the Jeep to take him back to camp. In the old days, I used to carry the deer out on my back, believing it had something to do with responsibility and respect, until my father pointed out to me that it was a good way to get shot, were I to pass by a fenceline and some other eager hunter who didn't know who and what I was.

The deer hang vertical from the same metal pole they've always hung from. There is art to the stripping, the paring down, no matter how familiar the act has become, over the years. We peel the neck cape back a bit to let the carcass cool and age in the mild November breeze, and then, a couple of days later, the deer is skinned, revealing every perfect muscle, every whitened strand of fascia. Creatures wrapped in muscle, red muscle sheathed within more muscle, sheathed then within more muscle.

I like some of it in chili. I like certain cuts of it in the iron skillet. I like certain cuts roasted, others breaded lightly in flour.

Taking them apart—first the long backstrap, which powers their sinuosity, then the shoulders, folding back like wings, with no joint to hold them to the body, only more muscle, and then the big hams, heavier than sacks of grain and fastened firmly with ball-and-socket, whose connective tissue must be cut; then the smaller pieces, butt steak and shanks and neck roasts. Neck loins, tenderloins, and then the delicate strips of meat between the narrow ribs. Then the flank steaks, the sheets of muscle transversing the ribs.

Now the deer is beginning to look more like a wingless bird or a reptile—all the vertebrae and ribs gleam. It's become such a shadow of its former self, and so light.

You cut and wrap, over at the butchering table, beneath the great oak. You toss the ligaments into the cedars, for the jays and coyotes to eat. For the soil, the cedar and oaks, to eat with their roots.

You might have a hundred pounds in your ice chest when you are done. Rendering the deer, you understand physically in a way you could not understand by reading or listening about it, that you are eating the mountain: that fruit trees grow fruit and that mountains grow deer.

The shape of those muscles you learned, in the disassembly, held silent discourse for you about the shape of the land that accommodated them: the gullies descended, the ravines climbed, the side hills traveled. Cleaning the deer, handling each muscle, you would stop and think how each muscle must have worked to travel across a certain feature on the landscape. And would again, in another.

Coming back apart the way we were assembled. Like the rocks, like us. As with the gone-away granite that formed and then laid down the crystals and then left, abandoning the crystals, so too are there ghosts of my family's deer all around. I see them, I taste them, and remember them across the years, and the places they were found. They are in the muscles of my arms, my back. They're in the cells of that part of the brain that holds memory.

WHAT HAS UNCLE JIMMY FORGOTTEN, with his stroke? Nothing, it seems; he just has great difficulty speaking or writing. He seems to remember everything. The little rifle that he and my father used to hunt with. The pig that chased him up the tree, gashing his calf muscle with its tusks.

This year at supper one night my father asks him if he remembers the big catfish that lived in the deep watering hole beneath the waterfall, below the old camp. I'd forgotten that fish myself—had forgotten it with a cleanliness and severity; there was a strange and not altogether unpleasant depthfulness to my forgetting, so that when my father's storytelling dredged it back up, I understood immediately that I would never, ever have thought of that fish again in my life, without his having mentioned it.

I was probably only six or seven, during the reign of that fish; it was long before I began hunting, though sometimes in the summer my mother and father would bring me up to the deer pasture just to walk around and to go on a picnic.

The catfish was a black bullhead, weighing probably more than ten pounds, and had lived in the clear deep pool below the falls since before I was born. The plunge pool was eight to ten feet deep, round and crystal clear, about the size of a large garage, and it was where my father and uncle and grandfather had bathed, no matter what the weather, in the old days, before electricity came to the Hill Country. The pellucid waters seemed to magnify both the brilliance of his skin as well as his size—this jet-black fish with whiskers like a dragon cruising slowly around and around, dark amidst the mossy green of the submerged boulders, and so *visible* in that clear water— and he was half-tame, so that you could swim next to him and around him in those clear waters, though he would shy away if you tried to touch him.

Then one year he was gone—any guess would be as good as another—and I was still a young boy, with a world to see and remember, and the memory of that fish escaped too, until it was brought back on this year's hunt, summoned by the memory not of my own doing, but of another connected to me.

"Yes," Uncle Jimmy says, when my father is done telling us, re-telling us, the story of that fish, "yes." Meaning: yes, he remembers. How strange it is that he is the one who has had the stroke but I am the one who has forgotten.

I HAVE BEEN TAKING photographs every year, and it's really starting to get fun now, as we knew, I suppose, it eventually would; I've been doing it for a long enough period of time, roughly thirty years, that the photographs are finally—after a long period of seeming timelessness—showing progression: aging, repetition, pattern. I have photos, unposed, of my father and uncle working on deer at the butchering table, and then, thirty years later, ourselves, doing the same work, and looking so much alike. As the photos of my father and uncle are now, like a dissolving magic trick, beginning to look so much like those of Old Granddaddy, thirty years earlier.

What's equally amazing is the realization that these patterns of repetition have probably been present all along; that it's only now, decades later, becoming evident, revealed to all, stripped by time.

It's amazing to me how meaningful some of those old photos are to me. Nearly indiscriminate snapshots—my father pondering a move in a dominoes game; Uncle Jimmy at the stove, spatula in hand, back at the old camp . . . . Things you never dreamed would be gone, things you never really considered one way or the other—like the existence of a big black catfish—but that now exist only in those pages.

The sight of them—like some familiar topographic relief—helps hold them firm in the memory.

Often now I find myself consciously taking indiscriminate photos of our surroundings, and our way of life at the deer camp, and of the landscape itself. Perhaps that's a code for the times: document the familiar. Even the mundane, the common, the secure, and the comfortable, will not endure. Sometimes you can't help but think that it's all already been decided: that there is no escaping, even if one wanted, the eternal relationship between a thing and the shadow cast by that thing.

THIS YEAR, MORE THAN any other, I was struck by how worn the paths are before us. The deer use the same trails; they scrape and rub the same trees with their antlers and, in the winter, shed their antlers in the same places.

Even the geometry of the world seems extraordinarily decided, some days. The curved, smooth-weathered silhouettes of the stones at dawn look like the curved backs of animals, haunch and hip, flank and shoulder, as do the rounded curves of cactus pads. Certain twists of branches look exactly like the branches of antlers. The similarity does not in any way diminish one's wonder at the reasons for and presence of life on this earth—if anything, it causes one to marvel even more. How easy it would be for our shapes to remain static, unanimated, even inorganic.

Just as visions, corners, flashes of grass in the wind swirl like the flagging of the bright tails of fleeing deer, but upon whirling to face that glimpse of sight, you see that there is no deer, was no deer, only wind.

NOT ALL THE GRANITE boulders come apart so quickly. A few are actually held together by thick mats of the bright hieroglyphic-patterned lichens that feed on the faces of the boulders—though they feed much more slowly than does the wind and rain. Perhaps this is what family is. We cannot stop each other's aging, and at times it must surely seem that the youth feeds on the parents, and the family on its past, wearing down a thing that once was. But the only thing more disintegrating would be to have none at all. And the lichens are like nothing so much as a depiction, with their strange roseate swirls and curlicues, of the vapors and currents of time's breath, but colored with such vivid hues—crimson, periwinkle, magenta, aquamarine, chartreuse—to be sure that we don't miss them.

Or perhaps if the lichens are not time, or family, they are stories and memory. *Something's* holding certain things together, while letting others fall apart.

ON THIS YEAR'S HUNT, a little miracle occurred, or so it seems to us. Uncle Jimmy shot a deer, a nice deer, an eight-point, over on the east side. It was to be the last and nicest buck we'd kill, on this year's hunt. He sat beneath an oak tree that afternoon of the next-to-last day, thinking and remembering God knows what—while my father parked about a quarter mile away, and waited, and watched the afternoon shadows lengthen.

About an hour before dark, says my father, the buck jumped the fence onto our property. My father watched the deer wander off into the woods in Uncle Jimmy's direction.

Uncle Jimmy can't tell the story. We really don't know what it was like for him when he saw the deer coming his way. How long he might have watched it before raising his rifle. Whether it spotted him at the last second. We know none of that: only that it was a good shot, a clean kill.

My father heard the single shot and went over to find Uncle Jimmy and his nice buck. My father drove Uncle Jimmy back to camp, then went back out to clean the deer for his older brother, as he and Jimmy had once cleaned deer for Old Granddaddy, in his waning years.

When I came into camp and saw Uncle Jimmy wearing his sweatsuit and sipping a drink, I wasn't sure what to think. I'd heard the shot and knew it had come from Jimmy's vicinity, but didn't want to just out and out ask the miraculous, *Did you get a deer? With one arm all but paralyzed, did you get a deer?*

Instead, I asked around the edges of it.

I heard a shot. Did someone shoot over there?

Yes.

Is there a deer down? Is that where my father is?

Yes.

Is he looking for the deer? (I imagined one hurt, wounded, leaving a blood trail.)

No.

Is the deer dead and down?

Yes.

Did *you* shoot the deer?

Yes.

MANY HUNTERS BELIEVE—have always believed—that it is not the skill of the hunter that brings game to the hunter—no human could ever be as wary or cunning as a wild animal—but rather, that the animal comes as a gift of the land: that it is an act of good luck, grace—a presentation. And that the good hunter always remembers this, and is always grateful, amazed by and marveling at his luck—at the beautiful, intricate specificities of it. And I'd have to agree: with every deer I've ever killed, that's always how it's been.

The mountain delivers a deer to you. Like something eroding slowly, the mountain shed itself of one deer, but sends it not randomly downslope, but in your direction.

It's easy to say thank you. It's the easiest part about hunting.

THE DEER PASTURE

THERE HAS BEEN DRAMATIC ecological change at the deer pasture, change in even the last hundred years. The old-timers, men and women of my grandfather's generation, and even my father's and uncle's, still recall the days before "cedar"—western juniper, *Juniperus occidentalis*—swarmed over the land, sucking the moisture from it, and creating a huge and escalating biomass of extremely flammable wax-coated fuel that one dry and windy day will burn hot and big, killing some but not all of the oaks (which are already being crowded out, killed, by the cedar, with or without a fire) and giving rise once again to sweeping grasslands.

The mountain above where we camp is called the Burned-Off Hill, known also on maps as Green Ridge, so named for the verdant pastures that bloomed there after the last big wildfire in the area, in the 1920s. For a long time afterward there were a ton of deer up there, huge herds that I remember even from my own childhood of the early 1960s, late-season herds of forty or more does, in which might be mixed a few spikes and one or two modest bucks.

Since then, as the cedar has reclaimed the Burned-Off Hill, the herds are smaller, but there are some bigger bucks, which brings us to a further discourse on change: how do you hunt deer in such a tangled thicket? Pretty much gone are the days of seeing deer wander across the wide savannah, canted into the wind like ships at sea. In the old days you could crouch in a grove of oak and cedar and watch such a clearing, particularly during the rut—typically the second or third week of November—and you could see some things.

Now, unless the cedar has been treated mechanically—dozed or cleared with chainsaws (though always, it sprouts right back, grows wildly, enthusiastically; only regular fire keeps it back)—there are fewer such openings, and the deer, particularly the bucks, have learned—not just as individuals, but as entire populations, via the filter of natural selection—to stay in the cedars as much as possible.

A thrilling way to hunt them now is to find a scrape or rub and sit in the cool shade of the cedar bower and wait. You'll hear the deer coming, their little hooves kicking against the loose granite and sandstone, and then you'll see, through the dense matrix of so many juniper branches, the tan shins of their forelegs, dappled in that latticed light. Then the legs will come slowly closer, down the little rabbit warren of a trail, and then, best of all, you'll see the glint of sun on a set of mahogany-brown antlers. You'll click your rattling antlers together, and blow once more lightly on your grunt tube, and sometimes, if you're lucky, the breeze will hold in your favor and the buck's keen bright eyes will not see you, will not meet your eyes (you'll be wearing a camo mask)—and when the buck moves again and its vision is obscured by a trunk, you can lift your rifle slowly and carefully and take aim.

It's more like hunting turkeys than deer. It's certainly not like it was in the old days, but it's fantastic; that part, the emotional core of it, will never change.

HOW QUICKLY, THOUGH, the rest of the world changes, and particularly once one is no longer a child! There is the far distance of the Old Ones—the exciting and yet also sobering feeling one gets upon discovering a perfect, or near-perfect, chip or arrowhead loose in the granite gravel beneath those slowly eroding giant hoodoo boulders—and then there is the nearer-distance of the old-timers who came just before my grandfather: the Byrd family, related to Davy Crockett, who was given this homestead in gratitude for Crockett's service at the Alamo; and old Homer Young, who married into that family, and from whom we first took our lease. (Howard married Mr. Young's daughter; after Mr. Young died, we leased from Howard.)

Our old-timers—Dad and Uncle Jimmy—still almost children, back then—recall that Homer Young would come down in the evenings to play dominoes, and even take a sip of whiskey, and seemed glad for the company.

Sometime after Homer and Mrs. Young settled, the cedar began to encroach, and for a while—half a generation, perhaps—a lone ranch-hand, working diligently and daily, was able, with a single ax, to chop down every invading cedar.

He could not have envisioned a world more different: the stuff of his nightmares, perhaps, as he considered his labors at the end of each long day, hands blistered, but with the cedar kept in check single-handedly, if just barely. One such laborer per ranch, holding back the weeds of the world and believing he could hold back change. But concurrent with his unknown passing, the cedar came, and still comes, an explosion of single-minded enthusiastic photosynthesis.

Because of this, the best way to hunt is to still hunt, whether during the rut or pre-rut, or in the harder times, following the rut. It's often hot as Hades in the early season, and rattlesnakes are often still active; in such heat, the deer seem to me to be even more crepuscular than normal. There's a tradition among many Texas hunters to hunt from high towers, in plastic blinds, over machines that spray corn out to the deer and turkeys, which then approach like domestic livestock. While it's not my place to judge another hunter, I have to say, that style is not for me—to my way of thinking, that changes the hunting to mere killing, and I see no need for that, here in the twenty-first century. As well, it's so wonderful to hunt a deer deep in the cedar thickets—again, it's like calling in a wild turkey, except that the deer has keen scent—that I feel a wave of pity for the hunters, or shooters, whose experience is so reduced by such a practice.

Sound carries, in the clean air of the Hill Country, and in November, hiding in a clump of cedar, waiting and watching, at daylight you can hear the mechanical whirr of feeders spraying corn pellets everywhere, followed by the almost simultaneous report of rifles near and far. I've had the good fortune to know the pleasure of wilder hunts—walking up on bedded animals, or waiting in the bedded areas, or sneaking through the boulders and catching them in pursuit of does—and it's all the difference in the world. I'd sooner go to the grocery store than sit like an office-hostage in a cubicle at daylight and wait for the mechanical farmer to spew corn and then, dutifully, the deer-turned-into-livestock to come galloping in. Call me old-school, but to me, there's a difference between killing and hunting.

MORE CHANGE: Back in the oil-rich 1970s, some Hill Country landowners began experimenting with the farming of exotic game animals—most notably axis deer and Aoudad (Barbary) sheep—with the Hill Country so closely resembling parts of Africa. Over the ensuing decades, the exotics have—as they always will—escaped their fences and are slowly establishing themselves in their new non-native habitat.

PERHAPS THE GREATEST change I have experienced is the strange circularity of no-change. I used to wonder if my father and uncle would ever one day take my grandfather's place as esteemed elder of the deer camp—such a time seemed light-years away—and yet somehow, through the turning of the calendars, it has happened. Just as strange, or stranger, to imagine my brothers and cousins and I likewise one day stepping up to inhabit that position.

THE LAND—THE RUGGEDNESS OF IT—has sculpted my brothers and cousins into good hunters. They've all killed so many deer, over the years, that they tend now to let them go, save for B. J., the youngest, who at thirty-four is still in full possession of his hunter's desire. (His birthday, the first of November, is celebrated at each deer camp; another tradition.)

There was a drought this year, like none that any of us have ever seen. B. J. was the only one who killed a deer, hunting it with his blackpowder gun, missing it, improbably, with the first shot, from a distance of only about fifty yards, but reloading (hiding, he said, behind the self-made cloud of blue smoke) and dropping the little buck, a second-year devil-spike, hammer-head-dead. It was good to have a deer in camp, and we were all proud of him and the old-school ways of his blackpowderhood, though in time-honored tradition we ragged him about the little buck's antlered inadequacies, and about that first missed shot, and we bitched and moaned when we each paid out the dollar tithe we give every year to whomever is fortunate enough to shoot the first deer of the camp, the dollar bills impaled on an ice pick thrust into the much-perforated kitchen cabinet above the old refrigerator.

The rest of us continued to act like old folks, walked the same thousand acres we've been walking for decades—knowing intimately every inch of ground—and spent more time remembering than hunting. Such is the luxury of our soft times, and such too is the blessing of wild country, to provide, even for aging hunters like ourselves, a place to do that remembering, as the world keeps changing, deciding in its ancient and graceful and inimitable way day by day what to carry forward and what to leave behind.

THE SILENT LANGUAGE

IT'S WINTER—December—and everything in Montana is buried beneath the heaviest snow in years. As with every year, but more so this year than most, I love the winter for itself, but also for the way it keeps nearly everyone else inside, releasing the woods to the gaze of only me and the deer, me and the mountain lions. I think about things going on in my mind, and then to recover my senses, when I get too lost or confused, I look at the woods.

After hiking in the woods all summer and fall, I find it hard to describe the feeling of how clearly all the pieces of the woods' puzzle come together in winter: knowing exactly what animals are in the woods by the tracks they leave, and what size the animals are, and where they go, what they do and what they eat, and where they lie down and rest.

The snow tells almost everything. The woods are silent, except for the occasional croak of a passing raven. The geese and ducks have headed south, and in the woods it feels as if you've been abandoned, and as if you're living at the top of the world—just you and the deer, marooned. Snowbound. It's lovely.

With most of the other animals in the woods, you already have a rough idea of what's going on in their lives. You see the deer and elk, moose and coyotes, almost every day.

The one animal you almost never see, however, that's up here year-round, is the mountain lion. It's a surprise to come upon their tracks each winter while out cross-country skiing, or walking in the woods, and find that they've been here all along, and closer than you could have imagined. (Once a lion's tracks went right up on my porch after a fresh snowfall, investigating around my cabin as I slept, perhaps having listened to my snoring from afar and come closer to see . . .) A mountain lion's big tracks are as easily distinguishable as any in the woods, and in the snow like that, they conspire to make you catch your breath and imagine the big cat stalking its prey, so silent with its big furred feet.

The tracks are beautiful, and when I follow those tracks it is always with caution and respect, as if I'm afraid of messing up the lion's stalk by coming up on it from behind and making too much noise, scaring away its prey, perhaps, or interrupting it mid-hunt.

No other tracks in the woods seem to have as much meaning as the tracks of mountain lions; always, they seem to be hunting. It's a feeling that seems to emanate from each pawprint. I always feel like I'm trespassing when I come across their tracks; I always feel like I'm somewhere I wasn't invited.

Stories throughout the West tell of how curious mountain lions are—of how they'll follow a man for miles, walking right in his footsteps, evidently just for entertainment. I have never backtracked in the snow to find the big fresh prints of a lion superimposed over my own, but occasionally—usually right before dusk—I've had the sudden *feeling* of being followed, or watched, especially in the summer and fall, when a lion would leave no tracks.

I'll turn around and look back, and will see nothing, though who can say?

A thing I like to do is watch animals, when I'm fortunate enough to see them in the winter without their seeing me. I like to study what they're doing, watch the way they're moving, and then after they've moved on, I'll go out in the snow to where they've been and study the tracks they made. I'll try and match what I saw them doing to what the tracks in the snow tell me. It's like learning, and listening to, a silent language. If you're not in a hurry—which I'm not—it's kind of fun.

Nobody up here gets in a hurry in the winter. I haven't seen anybody in a week. Three days ago a truck drove past and the dogs ran out barking at it, having forgotten that trucks had permission to do that—to drive down the road past our cabin.

I've got this great book, *A Field Guide to Mammal Tracking*, by James Halfpenny, and have been reading it—taking the little quizzes at the end of each chapter, after he shows an illustration of a set of mystery tracks. (What is this animal doing? What kind of animal is it? How old is this animal? Is this animal running toward or from something?) I will read from Halfpenny's book and then think about all the hours, the days, the years I've been fooling around in the snow, trying to learn the silent language of the woods, and it amazes me how long it can take a person to learn something when he or she tries to do it on his or her own, without assistance.

Like I said, I haven't progressed very far. But now I'm trying to be more careful. I'm paying attention to the claw marks at the tips of the tracks, to the differences between back and front feet . . . . It's nice, being out in the woods in winter—whether on skis or snowshoes or on foot—and I like the fact that the more silent it gets, the more frigid and austere, the more it helps my focus. Even though I don't see nearly as many animals in winter (they can hear me coming), I can still continue to learn about them. Even though I can hear nothing, they are still speaking to me. Because spring is a long time away, and because in winter I have all the time in the world. I can spend a long time traveling only a very short distance each day, following tracks.

A somewhat horrifying thing—but somewhat thrilling also—when you're following mountain lion tracks through the woods is to come upon a kill: the blood-red snow and the thrashed-out area; deer hair everywhere and a leg here, a leg there—a few bones and sometimes a bare skull. Coyote and raven mop-up tracks will cover those of the lion; no meat is ever wasted in these woods.

No other track in the woods, in winter, has for me such a lingering force as does the mountain lion's. I seem to be able to feel the *echo* of the lion's leap, as it caught the deer—biting the neck to strangle its prey, bringing it down and then tearing out the entrails with a strange burrowing motion. (I've found fresh kills with the entrails separated neatly from the carcass.)

When I am walking or skiing or snowshoeing in the woods in winter and come across lion tracks—especially at dusk—I try to walk bigger, to discourage any nearby lions, propping my arms out away from my sides, and I walk in ludicrous *yeti*-like steps that would make anyone who saw me hoot, but there is nobody, it's winter . . .

I've seen a lot of animals in the woods up here, and I have seen a lot of amazing sights—have been chased up the tree by a bear, have seen deer giving birth, otters playing in the river—but some of the things I haven't seen have moved me just as deeply.

I have seen two wolverines' tracks out in the center of the frozen river, heading resolutely north, upstream, the tracks crossing the international boundary, back over into Canada, as if disappointed with what they had found in the United States.

I've seen the huge pie-plate prints of a woodland caribou, up on Caribou Mountain, even though they're supposed to be extinct in Montana and down to only a dozen or so in Idaho, just a few miles to the west.

I've followed a set of wolf tracks through the woods too, near a cattle ranch along the river, back in the 1980s, when wolves were not thought to exist in Montana anymore. I saw where the wolf had stood on the riverbank and looked across the broad snowy pasture and then had turned and gone back into the woods.

So everything's out here, still, in the winter—except for the bears, who are sleeping like children. (I've heard that sometimes down in its snow cave a bear's warm breath will melt a kind of blowhole in the ice and snow, a hole going back up to the surface, and while traveling across the snow I look for such holes. I like to imagine the bears beneath my feet, curled up and sleeping in all that snow . . . . I've also read that if you find such a hole and put your ear next to it, you can hear the bear half-breathing, half-snoring, and that it is a sound described as "a tremulant hum" . . .)

It is a fine thing, is what I mean to be getting at, to be seeing all the animals' tracks so frequently, without seeing the animal. To know that a thing is still out there without ever really seeing the thing—just feeling its presence. To see the tracks but not the animal can yield a brief comfort sometimes when I am in the woods and grieving. Some moment will turn slightly, as with a screw. I'll sense some thought, some presence, some feeling, without actually hearing or seeing her, my mother, and while I do not understand it—my loss of her—I will know with rock certainty that she is out there, in a different way, a way I cannot understand.

I HAVE SEEN DOZENS of lions since I've lived up here. It is the second lion I ever saw that is most interesting to tell about. Two young girls and I were walking through a grassy meadow far back in the woods. We were going fishing. I saw the lion first, about fifty yards away, resting under the only tree in that meadow, looking back at us. The girls had been laughing and singing and I believe that the lion—a big one—had come to investigate their voices. The lion's head was as round as a basketball, with beautiful, round, mascara-lined eyes, it seemed, and cheeks smudged with charcoal blush. It looked like the face of a human, watching us. The grass was tall and all we could see was the lion's head, watching us back.

I thought at first it was just a deer lying in some odd position that made its face look like that of a lion. (It strikes me only now as startling that the lion and the deer, predator and prey, have the exact same color of fur.)

To tease the girls—to frighten them—I said, "Hey, look at that lion lying down, out there in the grass." I lifted them up on my shoulders—Amanda, twelve, and Stephanie, ten—and they said "Yeah, a lion!" They were thrilled, and I felt badly then and had to tell them that I was teasing, that it was just a deer looking at us straight on, in a manner that made it look like a lion—that it had its ears tucked back or something.

Just then the lion turned its head sideways, looking as regal as a queen, and I couldn't believe it, but there it was, right in the middle of the meadow. It was the meadow we had to walk through to get to the lake.

I'd read all the books. I knew that lions were leery of adults and would run from you if you approached them. I didn't want this lion stalking us. I gave the girls the canoe paddles and I walked out across the meadow, through waist-high grass, toward the lion, certain that it would come to its senses and bound away, once it saw what was up.

I kept walking—getting closer and closer.

And began to walk more slowly.

The lion kept watching me. When I was within about thirty yards—close enough to see the animal's eyes—I could see some flicker of interest, some curiosity, and more—intelligence—in the big animal's eyes. I knew I should turn around and go back to the girls and lead them on home, but I couldn't help it: I knew I could flush that lion into running away, and besides, the lion was drawing me on, as if hypnotizing me, and there was also the strange, foolish notion of territory; I'd been fishing this lake for six years and didn't want to be run off from my fishing spot.

But mostly, it was hypnosis that made me keep walking.

The lion looked left and right, when I went inside that thirty-yard perimeter—as if looking for another lion to consult on this odd behavior in humans. (*Coming right in to me,* the lion seemed to be thinking, *too easy!*)

The books said the lion would run away.

This lion didn't know that.

At twenty-five yards, there was an exquisite tension—and that is the only way I know to describe it, with the word "exquisite." The tension had been building as the space between us compressed, and the lion had been handling the strange compression beautifully, and I had been steady and unfaltering in my own approach. A relationship was forming between us, with no two other things in the world at that moment for either of us except each other—and I paused, so aware of the tension and compression of air that to take one more step would suddenly have been as freighted a movement, as nearly impossible, as if I had been wearing lead boots on the planet Jupiter.

I knew with an instinct, a certain knowledge deep in my genes, that if I took one more step that compression would shatter, and I would become in that instant predator or prey, and that the lion would charge me, or would run away. The lion knew this too. We were both suspended at arm's length—twenty-five yards.

I took a step forward, and the lion jumped up and turned and bounded away in a swimming, arching motion through the tall grass and into the woods at the other side of the meadow.

The girls were ecstatic when I went back to them; they had not felt the compression. They had only seen the lion run away.

"That was so beautiful!" Amanda cried. "A lion!"

"A *real* lion!" Stephanie said.

"You girls will remember this," I said, "the rest of your lives."

Euphoric—feeling privileged to live in such a wild place as to still be able to see a lion—we continued on through the tall grass toward the lake. We were following a deer trail through the grass, and at times the grass was taller than our heads, and the trail through the grass narrowed so that it was brushing our shoulders on either side.

When we got to the lake, we slid my canoe into the water and were about to get in when I looked out at the meadow and saw that the lion had come back and was closer than before—only about thirty-five or forty yards away, with that big round beautiful face, the head as big as a small pumpkin.

This time I was not hypnotized by the animal's beauty, nor was it (I could feel this) in a mood to fool around with any games of compression. The lion crouched low into the grass when it saw we had it spotted. We stood up on the canoe's thwarts to get a better view, and the lion sank lower still, disappearing completely in that sea of cool green grass, and then it did a strange and beautiful thing: it stuck its tail straight up into the air, its long black-lined tail as straight as a rod—held it stiff and straight like that for a moment—and it began twirling the tail back and forth, making it into the shape of a question mark, swirling it with a lazy, hypnotic seductiveness, trying to lure us out into the meadow.

We had gone to the lake to go fishing, but only because we were running late. What we had planned originally to do there was to play our favorite game—"Tiger in the Grass"—and had it not been so late in the day, that is what we would have done.

The way that Tiger in the Grass is played is simple. Stephanie and Amanda and I get down in that head-high summer grass and then begin crawling through it, growling, pretending to be tigers, crawling and parting the grass before us, growling all the while, until we hear someone nearby, and then we pounce and try to land on that person, surprising them: the "tiger" seemingly appearing from out of nowhere, so perfectly hidden, down in that tall sea of grass.

There is no telling which of the three of us the real tiger would have stalked and leapt upon, had we been down on all fours, oblivious, in that high meadow.

The reason I do not give the name of the lake is that I do not want hunters to go there with their dogs and hunt the lion. I was not smart—or not *thinking*, that day—but I will be ever after. The woods need lions. It was a thrill and an honor to see this one.

Nonetheless, it was now evident that we were being stalked. I gathered the girls behind me—it was nearing dusk now, and the lion had disappeared from sight completely, was somewhere down in that tall grass. I told the girls to talk in loud voices, deep men's voices, not children's voices, and we held hands and held the paddles and fishing rods before us and started back through the meadow, through the head-high tunnel of grass out of which the lion could lunge at any second, and I have never felt so fierce, so furious, so protective in all my life, and I knew then how a mother feels, for I love these girls dearly, and if the lion had jumped out I know that I would have throttled it with my bare hands before I would have let it get to them.

Like three-people-who-had-become-one, we moved slowly down the grass tunnel, and the girls were braver than anyone could ever have asked, saying, "Just go away, lion," and things like that, in deep voices, and I was saying pretty much the same.

The lion could have made an attack at any time, while we were in the grass. It knew that, and I knew it, and I think that the girls knew it. But we passed through the meadow in safety, made it back to the trail through the woods, and whether the lion followed us or not, we could not see.

I'll never walk through tall grass again without remembering that lion, and that day. Many people go all their lives without seeing a lion, but these girls got to see one before they were even teenagers, and I believe that special events such as that are like sterling, that there are only so many people blessed with such moments, and that those moments stay with them and shine within them, brilliant, while most of the other events of life fade with time.

LESS STERLING—more ephemeral—are the trails of deer through the woods in winter. I'm confused by what seems to be at first the paradox of my hunting them in November and then feeling great empathy for them as I fall out of the chase while they still labor on in the snows of December and January, trudging ankle-deep and then belly-deep and then worst of all, sometimes chest-deep, with never a moment to rest, never a night of safety.

Me, I get to lay the rifle aside and rest and become human again for eleven months, but the deer must keep going, must never rest, not even in the deepest snows or on the coldest nights, or the lions will get them, the coyotes, the wolves.

The woods up here seem simpler and more reduced in winter, but they're not. The snow's just what it seems: a blanket, hiding nearly everything, and letting it sleep. It's still as intricate a system as it ever was. The deer must walk the tightrope, as must everything else in the woods, of too-much and not-enough. A little forest fire, for instance, is good in the summer. It promotes fresh nutritious growth for the deer. But too much fire, as has been the case in recent years due to man's fire prevention policies (which backfire and lead to an excessive accumulation of "fuel"—dead trees that *should* have burned), is also bad for the deer, bad for the soil, which can get washed away by erosion following a fire, which is bad for the rivers, which is bad for man.

All of these variables are hidden in winter. The deer flounder through the snow, eventually packing down trails like highway systems through the woods. They experiment in December—cutting several trails before finally establishing a system by January that works for them, gets them to water and to feeding areas with the minimum expenditure of energy. Because I fear the terrible droughts we've had in the last several years, I am glad for every snowfall. "It's good for the country," I say, thinking ahead to the trickling, nourishing snowmelt of May and June, of wildflowers, of green rich July grasses. Too little snow can make an easy winter for the deer, but will assure them a very dry, hot, dangerous summer.

This year, however, I'm seeing what too much January snow can do to them—too much, falling too quickly. It will help make summer richer and easier—if they can survive that long. Too much snow covers their food (dry leaves and mosses), and wears down their fat reserves because it's so hard to thrash around in. Deer have tiny hooves, of course, compared to the big snowshoe feet of the predators—bobcat, lynx, coyotes, wolves, and lions—and in deep snows such as this year's, predators have the advantage.

So I stop hunting about the time the snow falls. But the deer do not stop being hunted.

Their trails through the woods—the further we go into the winter, the more worn-down those trails get. The deer use them every day, as does everything else in the woods—lions and wolves, predator and prey. The game, if one wants to call it that—though it is not a game; it is life and death—becomes much more focused. It would be like your trying to run from a pursuer, but having to stay only on sidewalks.

If the deer leave the trails they've created, and flounder in the deep snow, they're goners—*if* something's chasing them.

And yet, by January, in heavy snow years, all the food along the trails is eaten, and they *must* go off into the new deep snow, looking for new food, *cautiously*, always vigilant.

I like to think of them the way they are when I'm hunting them in November—fat, healthy, wild; not vulnerable, as they are later.

And yet, I love the predators, too—the wolves and lions.

And I love to see the snow fall, love to ski across it, and love the thought of how the deeper the snow, the lovelier the spring will be—"Good for the country," I say, every time it snows—but there's always that haunting ambivalence in my knowledge that after a while the snow can shut the deer down, can lead to their deaths in great numbers.

Never mind that it's all a part of a very fine-tuned, constantly correcting system of balance. Never mind that if I'd only remember my manners, I'd realize that I'm only along for the ride.

I still can't help it; I evaluate every snowfall, every day, with that odd mixture of satisfaction and worry—I get *involved*, as if nature cares one way or the other what I think.

The bucks drop their antlers in January. They've used them for territorial defenses in mating, and even for defense against predators, but by January survival has become such an iffy, day-by-day venture that they try and save every calorie they can and have evolved to shed the antlers to avoid having to lug that extra weight.

A thing I love to do in the spring, after the snow is gone, is to walk in the woods looking for the winter-dropped antlers of deer, elk, and moose. It is not unlike a naturalist's Easter egg hunt, in that from the antlers you find you can determine rough life histories—sizes, sometimes age, and even temperament, if the antlers have the battle scars of combat. But mostly I like to find them because they are beautiful. The full basketball curve of the main beam, and the splaying fingers of the other tines . . . the palm antler of the moose, and the immense elk antlers . . . . Finding the giant elk antlers is as incongruous and exciting as coming upon a beached whale in the woods. The antlers speak silently to last year's lives, which are now memories, and some not even that.

The most beautiful time to find a fallen antler is in an open stretch of woods late in the afternoon when the sun is dropping soft tiger stripes of light down through the cedars or pines, and one of those shafts of light happens to fall across the antler's gleaming brown polished curve.

Sometimes the antler falls right-side up, like an open basket, cradled in the leaves as if to hold light and air, and other times the antler falls with the tines sticking down, like a pitchfork, so that the antler sits like a dome. And then in the cedar jungle, in that end-of-day light, with all the vertical trees and the horizontal twigs and branches on the ground, and the near-horizontal sun rays, the incongruity of that beautiful curve there on the ground, and the beautiful burnished gleam of the antler, will leap out to the practiced eye. And it is a thing worth seeing, in this life, a moment of no small consequence as you come to the spot where a deer lost part of himself but kept on going, a kind of a parting of the ways in that precise spot where you're standing, and the deer went on into the rest of the winter, having jettisoned it all, and kept living for at least a little longer.

Deer grow new antlers each summer. I cannot grow my mother back, though I must say there are times when Mary Katherine looks at me with the same ice-blue eyes and I am confused, for they are as intent and piercing and beautiful as my mother's, and they seem to know things that my mother knew, my mother knows.

Like the deer, I must keep going—must not succumb to the snows of winter, which is when, a year ago, I lost her, and the snows of sadness, which is, I suppose, more what this essay is about than anything. There are days . . .

Because it has now become clear to me that I have all the time in the world—for grief moves like a glacier, and sorrow like a slow river, and even memories move slowly, like clouds in the summer that seem not to move all day—because of this, I have started looking for antlers in the winter, right after the deer have dropped them.

It doesn't matter if I find any. It is somehow the act that matters, the devotion to the pure improbability of it: like finding a contact lens that has been dropped out of a helicopter and into the ocean.

I want to find the antlers before the breach, the distance between loss and continuance—the deer moving on away—gets too great. I dream of seeing a deer with just one antler, having just dropped the one side and ripe to drop the second. I dream of watching the antler fall from the deer's head, being there to see it when it happens, and walking up to that spot in the snow, groping, and finding that antler, while the deer has moved off only a short distance and is still in sight, antler-less now, browsing the winter-dry leaves of alder.

I take my dogs with me, and I go out on skis. Sometimes we ski down the deer trails, further packing those thin highways through the woods, which will help the deer run faster when pursued, and I feel good that I may be helping them in that manner. It is on these trails where they often lose their antlers—ducking under a branch, the antler joint (weakened by a cessation of hormonal flow) wobbles, then falls, and the antler is cast off.

I probe the snow with my ski poles, listening for the *click*! of the pole's tip striking hard antler. My dogs are hounds, with hounds' keen noses and curiosities, and they have come trotting home with deer antlers they've found before, carrying them only for the scent. It is my hope—and only a casual hope or dream, for I have all the time in the world, so much time before me—that my dogs will scent the antlers beneath the snow whenever we pass over one and that they will dig down and discover it with their good hot noses.

But this is unlikely.

We ski and we look, and we get through the short days, the dogs and I. Sometimes we cross the lion's trail and follow it to the remains of a weeks-old deer carcass; the dogs dig furiously, and I hope at first they've found a dropped antler, but instead it turns out to be a whole deer, and usually it is a doe, no antlers, or a buck that has already dropped his antlers, and there is only a bald skull and hooves, hip bones, ribs, and vertebrae—no beautiful antlers, no prize in the woods . . .

Sometimes the dogs and I will cut new trails in the woods—the dogs floundering ahead of me, lunging like porpoises, half-swimming in the snow as they break new trail, with me following on the skis to help pack it down. We'll spend several days taking the same route, until the deer find it and begin using it. It's a pleasure to spend several days constructing, with only the strength in your legs, such a trail, and then ski it one day and find that the deer have discovered it, and to see all their fresh tracks on it where they have used it the night before.

I feel tender toward the deer in winter, and yet I do not grieve when I find where a predator has gotten one, or even when I find one that has starved, one that has used up its fat reserves in the deep snows and has been unable to find anything to eat. I'm sad and quiet, but I do not grieve.

Another quiet sight—but one that does not touch me all the way down, does not bring full grief—is to see the reckless dependence deer place, in a hard winter, on the random chance of a fallen tree. The black tree lichen, *Bryoria*—the old man's beard—grows high on all the branches of the lodge-pole pines, the Douglas firs, and the larches, especially in dark forests, which are usually dark because they're overcrowded, and when the trees are over-crowded they're more vulnerable to root-rot and pine beetles and other dis-eases and hence more likely to topple, to be blown over.

When they fall, they bring that previously unattainable *Bryoria* down to the ground. It is said that the deer start running toward the sound of a falling tree in winter the minute they hear it, though I have never seen this. I see such fallen trees alongside the road, however, and it's true, there'll be twenty or thirty deer standing around the fallen tree, chewing savagely at the *Bryoria*, a wispy lichen so thin and dry that a whole garbage bag full of it might weigh only a few pounds.

There is both a numbness and a desperation in the deer's eyes, in the coldest of winters, and some of them do not make it, and what amazes me (and I think of this on nights when I am in bed under all the hides and blankets and the thermometer drops to forty below, and the stars crackle) is the fact that *any* of them make it. They have nowhere to go, nowhere to hide, and yet they go on because they have to go on.

There is a rock that we ski past, a cliff wall over the switchback of an old abandoned logging road that we like to ski, the dogs and I, when going up on the mountain. I call it "Panther Rock." Sometimes when we pass beneath it (me skiing hard and fast down the steep hill and the dogs running hard, just in front of me), the dogs will suddenly come to a stop, whirl around, and turn their noses up toward the ledge above and growl and raise their hackles in a way that I have seen them do only for bears, but the bears are sleeping.

That's one of the ways a mountain lion hunts—to perch hidden on a ledge, waiting for quarry to walk by below. I think about what a tempting target I would make on skis, how I would probably look to a hungry predator like just another deer floundering (my ski poles looking like third and fourth legs), and me running from something, and almost helpless, almost a victim.

I have not seen the lion on Panther Rock, but I know he's up there. There are days when I believe that if I faltered, it would be within his capability to spring down and get me. Still, I ski past it, and sometimes right at dusk, because to shy away from it would be to also act like a victim, like prey, and I am confused in my sorrow, feeling some days angry and like a predator, but so many other days more like the deer, and I do not want to be a victim to my grief, and I respect the deer more and more.

SOMETIMES I SIT ALONE IN THE WOODS, without the dogs, and I just think. I remember things: I turn the sterling memories of her over and over in my mind, polishing them like stones. I'll think of just one day—sometimes a special day—a summer day. I'll sit there just breathing slowly, breathing smoke clouds, remembering it.

Then I'll get up and head on home, gliding silently through the woods, across deep new snow, breaking new trail, and I'll wonder if this is how the deer feel, trudging through all the snow with their heads down.

I continue to look at all the other various tracks and realize that I am learning what so many others before me have learned: that there is no sense that can be made of it, and that it is more frigid and painful and hollow than you ever dreamed it could be, and that you want to lie down and quit but that because you are hers you do not, and you keep going. You keep going, but in so doing it does not mean that you are either understanding or accepting, only that you are still going, and that also by your still going on you know it does not mean that you are leaving the winter behind.

A TEXAS CHILDHOOD

IT'S LATE JANUARY, and I'm sitting on the porch at the farm in South Texas again, watching Mary Katherine and Lowry, now nine and six, playing out in the middle of a pasture, surrounded by balmy breezes and birdsong— a week's respite from the Montana winter. After long-winter's accruing numbness, this premature burst of song and warmth rests upon all our skin exquisitely.

Watching the girls play, so far from the Montana wilderness, I find myself wondering, What, from childhood, informs us as adults? What images of nature—and what relationships—last? The physical memories of the world, surely, and yet also the fabric of stories. Both must make a child, and then an adult.

It seems a paradox to me that the more deeply physical senses are felt or otherwise engaged, the more deeply the mind can be stirred: as if these things, birdsong, breeze-stir, sunlight in winter, distant dog-bark, reminding me of my own childhood in Texas, are but story themselves. Occurring again and again in that manner, they are as strong, once the echo or memory of them exists in your mind, as they ever were to the original physical touch or sensation.

As a culture, we have been presented with the idea that a thing must be either-or. But isn't it a valid possibility that deeply felt physical experiences can act not as a trade-off for the more interior world of emotion or story, but instead as a gate or path into a deeper interior world?

For a long time I thought the two were oppositional: the physical senses versus the life of the mind, as if the two were engaged eternally in some giant tag team pro-wrestling match of winner-take-all. Like so many others, I fell into the trap of thinking we were separate from nature—that we had not been birthed from the dust, and that because of the size and complexity of our brains, we were the exception to any rule we desired to oppose or discard.

But these thumbs that we're so proud of—the ones we are so sure have led to such rapid advancement as a species, allowing us to pick up and examine almost anything—have acted like a shortcut to the experience of millions of years, gotten otherwise by treading through time (moving across slickrock domes with padded feet, climbing trees with claws).

The shape of our calves are but direct reflections of the shape of the earth that we walk across; our arms, spreading from the warmth of our chests, are like nothing but the limbs spreading from the trunks of the deciduous trees that must have flourished in the land and the time that existed when we were being born. Our songs, our fluted musical instruments, so like those of the cries of migrating geese, or the howls of coyotes, which, heard from a distance of only a mile or so, are nearly indistinguishable. And what is a mile to natural history?

Our hair like the prairie grass, our skulls like river-polished boulders.

A thousand touches, and then ten thousand, and finally one day—the thumbs lifting and examining and holding and possessing, until we arrive, not like an afterthought nor any crowning glory, but instead only as if *Yes, here is room for you, too, there is room at the inn . . .*

Perhaps if we keep touching things, keep experiencing the world—perhaps we are only ten million-million more touches away—we will someday muddle through all the present clumsiness—this polar ice cap-melting, Ebola-contagion, nuclear-pissing-match foolishness—and will become even more graceful upon the earth, even more fitted to the shapes of our magnificent mountains, our arroyos, our sand dune beaches, grasslands, wild forests . . . . Perhaps . . .

I was talking about *story*, which I have come to think of as perhaps little more than the electrical charge that exists—like sparks across a synapse—between touch and the processing of information gathered from that touch, on its way into the catalogue of memory.

If this is so, then everything is story and therefore for a writer or story-teller, there could never be a dearth of stories, only a dearth of time in which to tell them.

These tiles beneath my bare feet, my bare feet in January, for instance—I aim not to spend but a sentence or two on them, though even as I sit here watching our girls play out in the cow pasture (sitting on beach towels in lawn chairs out in the bright sun in caps and sunglasses and swimsuits), I am reminded, spark-like, of the story, the saga, of how these tiles beneath my feet got here.

My parents and my youngest brother B. J. had crossed the border and driven down into Mexico to buy the tiles more cheaply at the factory, choos-ing from the culls that had never been shipped to various ports—tiles of varying shades of salmon, tangerine, and sandstone red; tiles with little cat and dog and rooster tracks on them, from where various domestic pets had scampered across the damp clay of the still-drying tiles, after they were poured but before they were baked in the kiln. A penny a tile, or some-such.

All right, five or six or seven sentences.

They'd taken their old manure-speckled, slick-tired cattle truck across, rather than renting a flatbed, and had stacked it full-to-groaning with tiles. In the summer heat, and on the ragged roads, they'd encountered various flat tires, so that they kept having to off-load all those tiles, one by one, to change each flat tire.

When they finally got to customs, my father was in a vile mood. Under-standably, his trailer was pulled over to go through the special inspection line, where, after an hour or two of inching forward in the long line, it was finally examined, and he was told that it did not have proper papers: the trailer would need to be quarantined, and the manure he had brought into the country would have to be sprayed off, and the trailer disinfected. He'd have to wait until Monday or maybe even Thursday of next week to get a permit—it was a Friday afternoon—unless my father could produce some form of documentation.

The sagging trailer, with all its tonnage, was blocking the only lane through the customs-search line. One of the old bald-patched tires was hissing, as was the radiator. Another tile off-loading was imminent. The cars and trucks in line behind my father seemed to stretch to the horizon, like the scales of some glittering and unending reptile. Horns were honking.

"All right," my father said, handing the customs agent the keys. "You can have it. It's yours. I've had enough. Come on," he said to his family, "we'll walk across. I'm tired of it. I don't want the tiles anymore, or the truck, or the trailer. We'll just leave it all here."

Steam was spewing from beneath the hood now, and the radiator was singing like a tea kettle.

"*Wait*," the agent said, panicking now, refusing the keys. "Just go on."

They proceeded. It took another eight hours, and four more flat tires, but they finally got back home and eventually built their home and laid their tiles—and now, B. J., who accompanied them on that sojourn, at the tender age of seven, is twenty-nine, and a stonemason, comfortable and accomplished in the patient and rigorous discipline of stacking and unstacking, sorting and choosing and weighing and measuring, but that is another story; there can never be an end of stories, they travel in all directions, for all distances . . .

Which ones become the quarrystone below? Who knows what moments—what combinations of landscape and story—conspire to ignite the sparks of enduring memory?

What is the nature, the effect, of various landscapes upon such memories?

I BELIEVE, AS DO OTHERS, that there are lightning-spark transformative moments in our lives, epiphanies, in which the milieu of all of one's previous experience is illuminated into an experience more profound somehow than even memory itself, so that the event seems to have somehow always been within you, waiting only to occur, predestined, miraculous, and splendidly unique and yet in retrospect completely unavoidable.

Perhaps there are a handful of such deep upwelling moments in every life—and yet (as if with the patience of a stonemason), I want to believe deeply that the general background dailiness of one's life is as important, in the long run, as any of those key handful of defining moments that occasionally come from the reservoir of one's life to provide that sudden jolt of deeper awareness or even understanding.

WHERE I LIVE NOW, so close to the Canadian, rather than the Mexican, border still affects my daily life. What world, what values, will we protect here for our daughters, and what inspirations and knowledge will come from the fabric of the elements we have chosen to make available to them, here in Montana? How will their lives and interiors be shaped by their seeing, in all the days of their childhood, these mountains and their storms, these moose and wolves and eagles and bears? By helping me hunt and take and then give thanks for, and then clean and prepare our own meals from the forest—deer and elk and fish and mushrooms and berries?

How will it all add up for them—the day the wolf was in the yard, the day the mountain lion followed us, the day the golden eagle caught the goose in the marsh?

What is the sum of this daily appreciating, and even becoming accustomed to these things: not taking-them-for-granted, but being accustomed to them, until you become so comfortable with the shape of things that their presence in your life fits you like your own skin?

And further, in such a life of woodsy immersion, do the occasional childhood upwellings of grace—characterized chiefly by a sudden sense of profound *belonging*—manifest themselves differently for woods-children already accustomed to being surrounded by such beauty? Do moments of deep nature-epiphany really arrive only for children of the suburbs and the inner cities?

I don't know. Maybe it doesn't matter. Maybe a slow and steady braid of beauty is every bit as durable and powerful as any tiny cluster or bouquet of crucible-forged revelations. Perhaps in the end it's all the same, and there's little difference, in this regard, between a Houston suburb and a Montana wilderness.

I don't believe that, however. I believe it is more a testament to the strength and purity of the hearts of children that the epiphanies of the natural world's beauty can and will come almost anywhere, at any time, rising as if from below, and unsummoned.

I think also that such a phenomenon makes the presence of wilderness all the more important, not less.

If semi-urban or domesticated nature can deliver such profound change and power to us, then what mystery must reside and flourish in the seething woods and swamps and mountains that lie beyond the reach of our roads?

And if glimpses of grace can be seen by children in even the narrowest, vanishing wedges of semi-domesticated nature, then what store must lie at the source—available in such free and undiluted state as to perhaps be readily observed and deeply felt by even the jaded eyes and hardening hearts of adults?

"OF WHAT AVAIL are forty freedoms," Aldo Leopold wrote, "without a blank spot on the map? I am glad I shall never be young without wild country to be young in." It was more than sixty years ago, and if he were still alive, I'm curious as to which he would marvel at more: the fact that so much wild country has been lost, even as he noted the rampant pace and breadth of its leave-taking three generations ago, or the speed of time's passage. As if surprised, ultimately, not at the quantity of loss, but by the brute law of how damned fast time passes.

IN HOUSTON, in my childhood, there was a farthermost place I could get to by riding my bike down sandy trails for a mile or so, beyond the last road and beyond the last house, and then by traveling farther on foot, through greenbriar and cane and willow and dewberry, along the game trails that followed the high cutbank bluffs of the serpentine bayou: traveling several miles of bayou-bend oxbow in order to traverse a single mile on the map.

It was a style of physical discourse or engagement that perhaps impressed itself upon my way of thinking, even my way of sentence-making, and is still where I am most comfortable.

There was always something to see, and I didn't want to miss anything. Leopard frogs leaping from bluffs out into the muddy current below; giant softshelled turtles floating camouflaged in sun-dappled patches of bayou, their dinosaur necks seeming as long as those of snakes; primitive alligator gars longer than I was tall and as thick around as my waist, cruising on the surface like mysterious submarines; armadillos, again seeming as strange as dinosaurs, and more beautiful than any bronze or golden jewelry, hopping across the trail, alarmed by my approach; box turtles wandering through the forest; and flying squirrels, fox squirrels, gray squirrels, raccoons, and opossums scurrying up the trees . . . . Nine-lined skinks scampered across and beneath the dry leaves of oak and hickory, their tiny scrabbly sounds distinctive, sounding like the first few faint drops of rain upon those same leaves.

There were sometimes even deer, there on the edge of the bayou—what a shock it was, to encounter an animal larger than myself—and often, while I was running down one of those trails, running only for the joy of being alive, I would sometimes surprise any deer coming down those same trails, and in their fright, they would sometimes crash through the brush and hurtle down those steep banks and dive out into the bayou and begin swimming for the other side.

There was a lake back in those woods—a deep swamp, really, already in the first stages of eutrophication, but all the richer for it—that I called "Hidden Lake" due to the fact that I never encountered anyone else there, nor even a sign of anyone's presence—no stumps, no litter, not even any footprints—as well as for the manner in which one came to the lake: passing through an old-growth forest of pine and hardwoods, with no indication that the lake lay before you, until you stumbled right onto it, with the many gray-spar rotting hulks of dead trees that surrounded its black water reflection forming roosts for an aviary that was nothing less than astounding.

Great blue herons would croak their ancient cries and leap into the sky— sometimes in their haste the old rotten limb they'd been perching on would fall into the lake with a large splash—and wood ducks, which back then had been hunted almost to extinction, would leap from those same black waters in a spray and blur, squeaking their whistling alarm cries.

Best of all were the egrets—snowy egrets, as well as the cattle egrets: ghostly birds rising and flying through the forest, as brilliant white as was the water beneath them black, and with those birds' slow graceful departure mirrored perfectly in the still waters beneath them.

I went there almost every day after I got home from school—this would have been forty years ago now—until the roads began being built into it, bulldozers and chain saws and concrete trucks, and fluttering ribbons tied to trees that I knew individually. And just like that, over the course of only a season or two, the woods were filled with noise, and then they vanished.

I was moving into adolescence by that time, and probably would have had my attention diverted anyway, for a while—and in that regard, I never really had to grieve that loss, as I had begun to supplant it, even as the forest was being leveled and the swamp being drained. It could have been a lot more painful than it was.

And perhaps an even larger blessing was my failure to realize, for a long time, that I was part-and-parcel of that taking: that my weight upon the earth, which was and is more or less the equal to any of us in this country, was part of the very thing that was flushing those copperheads and box turtles from hiding and sending those deer crashing into the bayou, swimming for the other side, to the brief safety of the wilder country beyond.

It is the unoriginal and damning realization of the fact of my complicity—of all of our complicity—that has helped lead me into activism, I think: a response fueled really by nothing more complex then an awestruck love of, and reverence for, wild creation, mixed with what remains perhaps a child's naive and deeply felt sense of justice and injustice.

THOSE DAYS, I BELIEVE, were for me the braid, rather than the epiphany: the slow accruing weave that helped form a medium out of which future lightning-bolt moments could occur, once struck, once ignited. Days in which I became more fluent in the language of that which would speak to me, and had already been speaking to me, and would speak to me again and again.

I don't think any sort of woods-fluency is necessarily requisite for defining moments to occur. I think these illuminations of beauty are a far more universal phenomenon, one in which the order of the natural world, and the grace of our inclusion in it, is shown to us as surely as if drapes or curtains have been peeled back.

Instead of our requiring any sort of earned woods-fluency, I suspect that there are periods in our lives when we are susceptible—or sufficiently undistracted—to refocus upon the world and see deeper into its beauty. And whether such moments result from some cellular activity within us, some maturation, or some shifting hormonal processes, some new-forming variance in the profile of our blood chemistry, or whether these shining moments are dispensed to us from above, dispensed every few years as if from some great and largely impersonal cog-and-gear revolution of stars and time and chance and fate, I have no idea: I know only that they exist.

Why? Almost anything can be explained through the lens of natural selection. Even *love* can be diced and parsed into terms of evolutionary advantage. But not these shining moments. Are they flaws in the system? What possible reason can there be for these occasional moments in which we are shown, as if through a rent in the clouds, or a slot-crevice in the cliffs, or even a tear in the curtain, such fuller magnitude of the beauty in which we are immersed?

I can't begin to guess what the reason might be for such epiphanies. But I'm glad and grateful that they exist in domesticated nature, and in the rawer, farther wilderness, too.

IN TEXAS—IN HOUSTON—I milked whatever wildness I could from the faint patterings of creatures beneath the leaves, and from the high-above brayings of the migrating flocks of geese, always synonymous with weather changes, and from little more than the north winds themselves, which, though rare, would clear out most of the petrochemical haze that hung over the city like a glowing dome. I milked wildness as much from the ghosts of wildness gone-by, or from the imagination, as from any remnant essence of the thing.

I PREFER THE SLOW and enduring form of sculpting—a geological sort of pace that allows for rises and falls, mistakes and redemptions both, but with absolution and success in the end; a pace in which any and all clumsiness yields finally to something smoother, as if that clumsiness is finally transformed by time running across and around lives. It doesn't matter, does it, whether you get your hundred volts one day at a time or all at once?

So keenly felt is even a single volt of the world's beauty that often even that single volt feels to me like a hundred. I think I am drawn more toward the daily, understated devotional of staring out at a marsh for long moments at a time, or at a forested mountainside, than any search for high-intensity moments of illumination, simply because I'm not sure the husk of my body could hold up to the rigors of any amped-up intensities.

My girls are far flashier in the world—far more fitted to it already: bright and beautiful, and certainly deeply loved. What will their moments be? Which will influence them more strongly—the slow daily braid, the continuum of nature, or the curtain-parting moments of supreme revelation? It can't be controlled, of course, nor perhaps even observed, not even by them. Of my own defining moments in nature, only rarely do I ever remember being aware in-the-moment of thoughts as cliché as *I will never forget this*, or, *Wow, this is a revelation.* Even those highly illuminated moments sank deep, as if into a river, and it was only after I had gone on some distance that I understood what had happened: that those moments were foundational images, mid-river boulders that changed somehow the patterns of all the subsequent flow downstream.

A different braiding, then, as the divided currents merged again.

The moments cannot be set up in advance. Magic comes when it comes. Perhaps this is another reason I am more comfortable with the accumulated daily sweetness instead of the exalted once- or twice- or thrice-in-a-lifetime euphorias.

I can help lead the girls to those quieter places. No one can do magic, but any of us can show up for work each day, can lead children to the raw materials that, once braided, conduct the world's magic. Like apprentice workers pushing a wheelbarrow full of various quarrystones to the place where a master stonemason is working, we can gather and select and then ferry those individual days.

Beyond that, nothing—only magic. The laborers can only show up for work each day.

IN THIS VEIN OF WHAT can be controlled, or at least influenced, versus what can't, I suspect that ritual and tradition are almost like quarrystones, or volt-moments, in themselves and that rituals or traditions undertaken in the out-of-doors can possess the same strengthening power—the same trans-formative ability, the same integrity—as the stones and antlers and feathers themselves.

The cross-country ski trip we take each year up the long ridge to cut a Christmas tree, the campout at a mountain lake each summer, the camp-ing trip into the backcountry each October, when the larch are turning gold, and when some years the snow is already falling. . . . These and a hundred other traditions exist for us already, some indoors and some outdoors, and they form a constancy, a security that I feel certain is good for children, and which, in these astoundingly fluid times, is probably pretty healthy for adults, too.

I don't mean to compare and contrast indoor and outdoor traditions; con-stancy is constancy. I don't mean to pit the minimalist against the maximalist. But I believe there is substantial value to our imagination in having the op-portunity to hike up a long ridge in the autumn, through all that quick color, and upon reaching the top—sweating, in the dry October sun—to witness the same scene magnified unending, an uncut larch forest of complete gold, and mountain ranges stretching to the horizon, and—in the imagination—perhaps farther.

The imagination is a phenomenal thing, a spectacle in its own right; by squinting just so, you can look at a birthday cake until the glimmering can-dles waver and appear to be the tops of golden trees, swaying in the breeze—but eventually you've got to open your eyes again, and see what's real and what's not. A cake's a cake. A mountain range is a mountain range. We can bake cakes. We can't make mountain ranges.

The scale of the backdrop of nature—particularly of wilderness—encourages and instructs us to see large, think large, dream large.

MAYBE YOU SEE ONLY what you want to see. Maybe we have the ability to almost always find what we are looking for. But the other day, I had not been thinking of these things—the illuminating moments of childhood—when one seemed to pass before my youngest daughter, Lowry, and me, rising not from the buried humus of centuries below us, nor from the braid-and-twine of the blood within us, but passing before us instead like fog—the fog-cloud migrating slowly, in the manner of an animal moving through the woods—a moose, perhaps, or a bear—and intersecting, that day, with our own curious wanderings.

It was a rainy day in January, raw and ragged and dark. The old snow already down was the only light in the world, and even it was dull. The moss hanging from the trees was sodden, and it was one of those days when dusk seemed determined to arrive two hours early.

The girls were home from school and were hanging out on the couch, eating slices of apples and slices of cheese, watching some movie on the video—*The Princess Diaries*, or something like that. I can't remember how it happened. Mary Katherine might have discovered she had some homework undone, but Lowry and I ended up going outside to ski for a while. I have to confess, I kind of forced the issue—something about the comfort with which they were ensconced alarmed me, the fact that they had not been outside all day, and that dusk was coming on—and there might have been a little of my own winter-craziness at play too, for I ended up issuing a mandate, a proclamation, acknowledging to Lowry that while, yes, I understood she didn't want to go outside, it was going to be a requirement, this rainy day, that we go outside for a moment, even if only fifty yards up the driveway. That it was for our health, and to break the braid, the pattern of the couch.

I don't know why I felt we had to get out that one afternoon. Certainly, other days have passed—rainy, foggy, drizzly days in the winter—in which none of us venture outside.

But this nearing-dusk day I was agitated. It didn't seem that I was asking too much. "Fifty yards," I told her. "I know that you don't want to go outside today. We'll come right back in. But we have to go fifty yards up the driveway. We just have to get out for a minute or two. We don't even have to have fun," I said. "Think of it as work—like emptying the cat litter, or something."

Maybe this was shaping up to be a train wreck. *Cat litter* equals the *great outdoors*? What surer way to dull a child's innate curiosity and even enthusiasm for the natural world? Had I snapped, in the seasonal deprivation of light, and turned into one of those awful eco-fascist parents? How was this dictum any different, really, to a six-year old from forced wind sprints, or a hundred push-ups? Dad the drill sergeant.

I'll tell you the truth, there were a few tears as Lowry got up and turned the movie off, and then pulled on her snow pants, and laced up her cross-country ski boots. "Why do we have to go fifty yards?" she asked—a very valid question—to which I answered, "We just do."

Maybe I was feeling something after all. Some summons. Or not. What does it matter?

Lowry stamped outside. She can be more obstinate than a mule. She can be more obstinate than me. *Why*, she asked again, and now that I had her outside, into raw nature this nasty, foggy day—now that we had broken somehow the cycle of the couch, where, now that I remember, she had spent the previous afternoon also, I was able to negotiate downward, and said, "Okay, you don't have to ski fifty yards, I'll pull you in the sled for fifty yards."

She dug in further, sulked deeper. She's not one to negotiate. Was I going to have to physically lift her in the sled? "Oh, *wah*," I said, "please, Daddy, don't pull me around in the sled, please don't make Princess ride in the sleigh, oh, *wah*." For a moment she started to giggle—it was enough for me to lift her in—but then she folded her arms and the Great Lip came back out.

"*I don't want to go*," she growled, and I felt like I had gone too far, and yet I felt I had made too much about it—the importance of getting outside for a breath of fresh air, even if only for a minute—to back down. I felt as if I had presented her with a choice, at least—skis or sled—but that I had gone too far. So far that I certainly couldn't turn back. The child-rearing books, I knew, would have all sorts of lucid and correct advice, but that didn't do me any good, for Lowry was already in the sled.

We started up the driveway, into the gloom. I pointed out the fifty-yard mark. She pouted and griped the whole way, milking her full fifty yards' worth. My God, how I hope she ends up on our side; how formidable an adversary she would be on the other side.

At the fifty-yard mark, I turned around, true to my word, and began running down the steep hill, and finally, that broke the ice-shell, the plaster cast of displeasure, and as she laughed and then asked me to do it again, I felt like an alchemist or magician.

It was the most amazing feeling: as if I had held her unhappiness cupped in my hands, and had done some trick—rolled it around for a moment as if mixing dust and water to make clay—and when I opened my hands again, there was happiness, where previously had existed only unhappiness.

It wasn't me, of course. It was the woods, and the earth—the slope of the hill, the laws of gravity, and so forth—and the condition of childhood, which seeks so earnestly, relentlessly, joy—but it was wonderful nonetheless to be witnessing it, and participating in it.

I pulled her a few more times, and then, truth be told—raging hypocrite!—I began to long for the warmth of the woodstove, the winter cabin light of hearth and home. Lowry was all bundled up, but I had neither coat nor gloves, having been certain we would travel only fifty yards.

Each time I suggested that we head back inside, she coaxed me into one more run, but then, finally, when we truly had made the last run, the one-more after the one-more after the one-more after the one-more, rather than going inside to warm up (*hot chocolate*, I urged her, and *Harry Potter*), she became absorbed by the myriad of deer tracks stippling the snow in the driveway: the regular herd of half a dozen (twenty-four hoofs) that wanders down the driveway at various times of the day.

There were tracks everywhere, traveling in all directions—days and days of tracks—but Lowry, with her typical singularity of focus, seized upon one track among all the hundreds of others, and then began following it, hunched over like Inspector Clouseau.

As best as I could tell, she stayed with it, too, parsing out for a little while that one deer's tracks among so many others, identifying it by size and shape as well as smoking-gun freshness, the blue-glaze sheen of that one set of tracks among dozens possessing a slightly brighter glow. Soon enough, she was tracking in a wandering maze of tight little circles, with me behind her, so that seen from above, our path would resemble that of these little teacup-bumper-rides in amusement parks.

It was nearly full dusk now, and darker still farther into the woods, and again, now that my goal was accomplished, I kept wanting to quit and to go back to the house and call it a day, even as Lowry was growing more and more engaged with following those tracks.

What it felt like to me was that something around her was unspooling—that if I had had her on some sort of psychic leash, it suddenly no longer applied, for whatever reasons—and so I followed behind her, careful not to comment or correct her, letting her believe instead she was hot on the trail of that deer, stalking it, inch by inch and foot by foot, and that we might come upon it at any moment.

So lost was she in following the one set of tracks through the maze—traveling in slowly widening circles—that I felt certain she had lost track of time and was so totally into the tracking that in her mind we had traveled miles, rather than continuing to circle back to more or less the same starting point.

Eventually, however, the circles widened enough that we found ourselves coming nearer the marsh, and as if still believing she was following the same deer, Lowry left off her circling-style of tracking and began following the tracks on a line, like an eager hunter closing in now, having solved both the riddle and the challenge.

The deer—still one among dozens, or hundreds—traveled, according to Lowry, down toward my writing cabin, where it circled my cabin before heading off farther into the woods, with so little light remaining now.

Do I know for certain that Lowry was entranced—illuminated—during this strange trailing, this impromptu, wandersome exploration? Not at all. And even during the traveling, the thought had not yet occurred to me. It was only when we heard the eerie whooping dusk cry of a pileated woodpecker, and she took my hand and led me to a clump of winter-bare alder, and hunkered down into a hiding position, that I began to consider that she was deeply in another world—or rather, deeply in this one.

"If we hide," she said, crouching behind a slender tree, "maybe he won't see us. Maybe he'll come closer."

The woodpecker called again, from high above, and not very far away, and Lowry pressed herself in closer against the spindly little alder and motioned for me to hide myself better.

We watched intently, waiting for the woodpecker to show itself. I could feel Lowry's focus, patient and keen, and I marveled at the purity of her desire. She didn't want to trap or hunt the bird, or even sneak up on it: she just wanted to see it, and to watch it, unobserved.

There was no way we could hide sufficiently behind that bare little alder, but Lowry didn't know that, or didn't believe it, and we waited longer, watching and listening. It was only when we finally heard the bird call again from much farther away, and with a deeper dimness—almost, but not quite yet, true dark—that we rose from our crouch and began walking back up the trail toward the house, with Lowry leading the way, excited and fulfilled, with the tears of less than an hour ago completely vanquished.

So strange was the turnaround in her mood and demeanor that I wondered if the woods-euphoria hadn't somehow been set up by the chemistry of the tears, allowing her to feel the day more sharply.

Goofy thoughts, I know. But she seemed so self-assured, curious and confident both, that foggy dusk, that I couldn't help but wonder if the images of the day weren't etching themselves indelibly upon her, like light coming through a brief lens opening to expose itself to the waiting film within.

There's no way to tell, of course, other than to one day ask her, far into the future—to see if that memory has withstood the test of time—and it may be that she won't remember at all: that the moment was not for her the vertical illumination of light that I imagined I was witnessing, but instead simply more of the regular daily braid of her life; that the moment was not a landmark pivot point, a boulder emplaced in the center of the river's current, forever after influencing all downstream flow, but that it was instead simply the river itself, always flowing.

My point being that none of it can be controlled.

And again, perhaps it is this simple: how powerful, natural, and necessary it is to our imaginations that that wild and rare bird had a place to fly off to. It just vanished from sight and hearing, when it went off deeper into the woods. But it didn't really vanish. It—and our imagination with it—kept going, drawn on farther and further and gracefully, into the wild.

MAYBE THIS IS WHAT I'm getting at, working my way toward it in much the manner of Lowry trying to parse out those tracks, making wider and wider circles—glimpsing the one path, then losing it, picking it up once more, only to have it vanish into the brush again.

Wilderness is not necessary to develop a love of nature in children. I'm convinced we're born with a reverence for the natural world and that that affinity can then be strengthened, maintained, corroded, or buried—like anything else in the world.

The joy, the realization or remembrance of that love, can be stimulated by one ant, one sparrow, one seashell held to one's ear. In this regard, the pastoral can be as powerful as the wilderness. But wilderness is still the long-ago mother of the pastoral and occupies a critical place in our imagination, which is one of the things that most defines us as humans.

Without wilderness, we ultimately compromise our ability to imagine further.

Without wilderness, we ultimately become less human. Whether we like it or hate it or are indifferent is beside the point: we need wilderness.

Surely there will almost always be ants, geraniums, deer tracks, and bird calls for children to ponder over and be smitten and captivated by.

But they should have the choice—should retain the choice—of being able to decide whether to travel even farther and further then, with that love, and that imagining, if they so desire.

We should all have that choice. It is, and should remain, one of the tenets of our culture, and one of the spiritual as well as physical riches of any great and powerful civilization.

BACK AT THE FARM, the wild Montana girls are sitting in lawn chairs, out in the cow pasture, feet propped up, wearing their sunglasses and swimsuits, beach towels over their shoulders, books in hand. The only sight more surreal to this image than the scraggly bonsai-reach of the thorny limbs of the weesatche and gnarled mesquite trees around them is the endless anthill-like mounds of manure, the scattered horse pods and cow pies.

But there's space, a comfortable amount of space, and there's also the exquisite luxury, to our Pacific Northwest psyches, of sunlight in the winter. A physical model, perhaps—that yellow light pouring down upon us—for how it is in our interiors, on those unmappable but deeply recognizable moments when that larger grace, and the hint of a larger understanding, or at least a larger acknowledging, pours down upon us.

Will these vacation days spent in another, more pastoral landscape, become some of their illuminating moments—and if so, how might that affect who these girls become, as opposed to the daily and nightly presences of mountain lions and bull elk?

Again, only after we have traveled farther downriver will any of us be able to pause and look back and remember, or not. But once more, the answer seems clear: we need as many natural places—as wide and diverse a mix—as is possible. Whatever the wild or natural world has, it is part of who we are and always have been, as well as who we are becoming. And that as we lose those various landscapes, we run the risk of becoming ever more brittle, until one day our imaginations and spirits might be as barren as a gully in a dry land, through which water once murmured, and alongside which cool shade trees grew, but no more.

You don't have to go down to that river—you don't even have to like such rivers—but we must retain them in our culture, all the different kinds of nature, and we must afford the most immediate and secure protection to the rarest kinds—the fast-vanishing big country, the gold standard of wilderness.

I was speaking of children, earlier in this essay, but now I understand that I am speaking to and of myself, and of the person I have become, and of the child I was, of one of the various paths that have opened before me, and that I had the freedom to choose.

TRADITIONS AND RITUALS, then—secure, predictable, and repeating—can be their own kind of vertical structure upon the landscape of who-we-are and who-we-become; and the repetitions or constancy of traditions can be like currents influencing boulders emplaced midstream, allowing for growth and complexity and creativity and movement downstream. It sounds at first like a paradox—how can something identified by its quality of *sameness*, of unchangingness, bring forth the fruit of change and spur the imagination?

But to know, or believe, that there are places in the natural world that are not likely to change too dramatically in a lifetime, harbors and refuges against the world's dynamic essence, can be a powerful and vital force that helps shape the growth of a child, and even the continuing growth of an adult.

SO TRADITION CAN BE A landscape unto itself—and story, or memory, can be like another of the physical senses, as deeply felt as any touch or odor or taste or sight, as deeply felt as any intuition or song.

Imagine, then, please, the sweetness I encounter on those occasions when I am able to bring my Montana girls out of the wilderness and down to the same pastoral landscapes I inhabited at their age—the pastoral farm, with its muddy stock tanks to fish, rather than high, pristine mountain lakes, and then, later in this vacation, to the deer pasture itself, the one-time ultimate arbiter of wildness, to a young boy, but a quantum step down, in wildness, to these girls.

Imagine the wonderful disorientation I feel as we arrive there at night, with jackrabbits bounding in front of the beam of our headlights, zigging and zagging in all directions as Mary Katherine gets out to open the gate.

The same scents, the same sounds, and even the same stories, there at the camp house that night. We build a bonfire of cedar in the same firepit and sit outside looking up at the same stars, and despite the fact that the lions and bears and wolves and jaguars are gone, it is still its own kind of wildness, to me, if not to these girls; though I can also say truthfully that if the farther horizons of Montana's wildernesses no longer existed, this place, too, and even its stories and traditions, would lose some of its wildness, wildness finally seeping out of this place, and all the other ones like it, in the manner of blood trickling from a wound that will not heal.

The sameness of security of these things allows us—encourages us—to change: to grow and reach and stretch, to dive deep and travel far. To go away, and to return—becoming as shaped, in our travels, as any of the other enduring shapes in the world.

The child standing next to a creek in the fog with a flashlight, peering down through the ice at a school of translucent, suspended fish, appears little different, thirty years later, from the young girls stalking along that same creek, trying to sneak up on, with their own flashlights, the night frogs and crawdads.

A clamant wildness, irrepressible, running beneath the surfaces, and across the surface, and just above the surface. A wildness in the heart of the farthest roadless area; a wildness in the sight of a single butterfly in a suburban backyard. A wildness in a single story, told or dreamed or remembered.

We need it all. We do not have to go looking for any farther or further wildness, but we need to know, or at least be able to imagine, that it exists. We need to be able to at least hear the echo of where we came from, even if a long time ago, and barely or dimly remembered now.

We need the dream of such a past, and the promise of such a future.

The green pastoral meadows sculpt us, the city parks and gardens sculpt us, and even now, the last few blank spots on the map sculpt us. It is all but one continuum, and we need it all, and our children deserve the possibility of it all.

And for those such as myself who have had the privilege of experiencing it all—high nature, low nature, city-garden nature, as well as the deepest wildernesses—it is this richness, this bounty, that inspires me to work for the protection of the rarest and most imperiled type of nature—the unprotected wildernesses, such as those that remain in the Yaak and other places—so that hopefully such a choice might still be available, in all the years to come beyond this one. All the generations not yet born, but coming, almost as surely as time itself.

COLTER'S CREEK BUCK

ONE YEAR, HAVING RETURNED to Texas for the Christmas season, I went back up to the deer pasture for what had once been a more common event in our family, which we called "the second hunt." In the old days, my grandfather and his sons had spent many New Year's Eves at the deer pasture, making a second hunt and welcoming the new year in that manner; though perhaps understandably, subsequent generations of us, somehow seeming to possess less leisure time have found ourselves hard-pressed to accommodate such an indulgence.

Beyond the icing-on-the-cake nature of going back a second time, the second hunt carried with it as well a cachet of wildness, in that New Year's in the Hill Country was often when the fiercest, most inclement weather passed through, yielding occasional freak snowfalls—one of the rarest of rarities, and offering us the seldom-experienced opportunity to try to track our quarry in the slushy snow for those few hours before it melted. (More frequent were the violent and beautiful ice storms, which dragged down phone and power lines and shellacked the entire Hill Country with single-digit temperatures and cast a sparkling diamond glaze over every rock, tree, and road, and gave the juniper-tinged air an even sweeter taste than usual: ice-scrubbed air so fresh and clean, at those temperatures, that it seemed to reach farther into the lungs, providing more oxygen, more sustenance.)

It was the same year that I had brought my amazing bird dog down to Texas with me—Colter, a liver-colored German shorthair pointer, a great ground-covering big-headed sweet long-legged bomber of a hound with nitroglycerine running through his veins—so that I could travel the state south to north with him, hunting bobwhite quail in the brush country down near Corpus Christi and in the highlands up along the Colorado River. It was such a good year for quail that there were even large coveys of them in the Hill Country, and in my young man's way, it was my intention to hunt them at the deer pasture, during my second hunt, before continuing up into the country on the upper Colorado.

In my mind, it was wonderfully rich and simple, if not excessive. I would hunt deer in the late afternoons and foggy, icy early mornings, then come back to camp midday for a warming meal and a fire, and take Colter out into the russet tallgrass to look for quail. It was dove season, too, and if I was lucky, I might have a chance to gather a few doves for dinner. Then I would return Colter to his kennel, put my shotgun up, and head back into the hills with my rifle, to sit on a rock ledge in the waning of the day to watch for deer. It was the year that my mother had died young after a long illness, and I have no doubt that in addition to my youthfulness, it was my relationship to the natural world, which was to say at that time chiefly as a hunter, that I turned to in part at least for grounding and support in this newer, lonelier, turned-upside down world.

It was painful, hiking those beautiful red granite canyons and sitting on those whale-gray ancient ledges of Cambrian sandstone, looking out at the same sights she had known and loved, though it was tonic, too, knowing that in the witnessing and the experiencing, these things were still shared between us, and always would be.

The first day, New Year's Eve, hadn't quite gone the way I'd intended. The evening before, my middle cousin, Randy, had driven up too, bringing his then-young son, Nathan, along with all kinds of items for our version of a New Year's Eve revel: no fireworks, nor cases of whiskey, but big fat free-range steaks, ears of roasting corn, fresh butter, green olives, giant baking potatoes, eggs, cream, sugar, coffee—enough food to stay a week, instead of just a couple of evenings. We didn't get to hunt much that first day, however, because we spent the day digging Randy's big pickup out of the mud. It wasn't really even mud at first, just soft soil beneath the litter of dark slick rained-upon oak leaves. Randy had left the gravel roadbed, was turning around to head back to camp for something, and had tried, inexplicably, to take a shortcut through the woods, where he quickly became stuck not just up to the axles—the usual barometer for such mishaps—but to the frame itself, so that he and Nathan had had to roll the windows down and climb out, unable to shove the doors open against the force and mass of so much mud, which had been rained upon almost ceaselessly for the last week.

Even from a distance, I could see the big blue truck—or the top half of it—when I came walking through the cold gloomy woods later that afternoon, with the steady rain still falling. As I drew closer, I could see the dark silhouette of Randy, barely visible in his rain-drenched camouflage amidst the dark trunks of the oaks, wielding a shovel, up to his ankles in soupy red mud, working as a farmer might labor in the stalls with his pitchfork.

He looked haunted, hopeless, mindless. He had been working for hours to no avail, for each shovel of slurry he pitched away was replaced within seconds by the porridge-like flow of new material from the freshly opened perimeters of his excavation, and perhaps most dispiriting of all, he could see none of his "progress," for the entire operation lay beneath the mask of the slowly broadening milky-red lake of his making. He could hear the gravel and mud scraping against his shovel, could feel the leaden weight of it each time he lifted a dripping load of it, but could ascertain no progress; when he saw me come slogging in from out of the rain and gloom, his mud-streaked face brightened, he actually smiled a half-grin, and wordlessly, he handed me a second shovel.

The sides of the big truck were smeared with mud, as if it were a wild animal that had been chased there before finally being brought to bay—a short distance behind the truck, there were twin tracks of deep-standing water that reinforced this notion—and from inside the mud-splashed fuselage, and through the rain-streaked windows, as if in a French fine arts film, Nathan peered uncertainly, his face brightening too when he saw I had come to join them. In the fading light, he was bathed with the blue glow of the little portable VCR with which he and Randy sometimes traveled, the machine plugged into the cigarette lighter. (I was to find out later that Nathan had been forced by circumstance to endure seven consecutive showings of *Teenage Ninja Mutant Turtles*, a fact that would ultimately sour him on that which had once been his passionate favorite.) Nathan smiled, waved wanly, and from the dry captivity of the interior, continued to watch, with the sight of us shivering and steaming in muck that was now knee-deep evidently more interesting than an eighth showing.

Trying to use my little sled of a rent-car to pull the truck out was completely out of the question, as was calling in a tow truck from Johnson City, seventy icy miles away on a fast-gathering New Year's Eve; indeed, the nearest pay phone was nearly twenty miles away. It was root hog or die, and strangely, or not so strangely, I was nonplussed by the size of the task. As much as anything—more than anything, perhaps—it grounded me in the moment, was both emblematic of and yet an escape for the grief and absence I'd been feeling all autumn and winter, in that first year of my mother's death, and would feel for a long time after.

Even the act of walking around searching intently for a deer in this beloved landscape, intimately familiar to me since childhood, had at times left me unable to hold back or adequately process that enormity of loss; similarly, despite the tonic of nature, the reality and permanence of my loss—the alteration in the relationship—kept coming upon me as I sat quietly in the woods, focusing on the hunt, or focusing on not focusing, which is sometimes the best way to hunt.

This, however, was not a moment of sadness, nor cause for complaint. So what if we were wet and cold? I was relaxing at one of my favorite places in the world, I was young and strong and healthy, I was with some of my family, I was uncompromisingly in the midst of raw nature, and in this particular moment my life had a focused and immediate purpose. It was all nothing but good, and I worked with pleasure, and slowly, Randy's attitude recovered, until, by the time darkness fell, we were working in concert.

We were not making any progress: beneath us, we could continue to feel the walls of our mudpit oozing to fill back in with the quicksand-slurry whatever we managed, with our aching backs, to export. Inside the darkened truck, the blue light of the VCR came on again—though still Nathan turned away and peered back down at us from time to time, as if to reassure himself that the truck would sink no deeper.

Somewhere down in the mire, there was a jack—in addition to trying to dig out a new lane, like the exit ramp from a subterranean parking garage, up and out of which we might one day—perhaps tomorrow?—be able to drive, we were attempting to hoist each wheel free of the muck's embrace, just high enough to place a flat stone, or a laddersticking of branches, beneath each tire, to help give traction at that point far into the unknown future when we might deem our endeavor sufficiently advanced to hazard a try at driving out.

So deep-sunk were the wheels, however, that we were having to kneel on all fours to reach beneath them, and even then we found ourselves working in water and slurry up to our necks, and then our chins, and then our noses, tilting our heads sideways, straining to shove a flat stone into the breath of space between tire and temporary bottom-muck; and again, hearing us thumping around beneath the truck, Nathan peered down anxiously and studied without comment the assemblage of various-sized sticks and branches that kept popping to the surface and floating all around us like so many circling alligators.

It was getting colder, and with nightfall, Randy pulled out his ever-trusty Coleman lantern and with shaking, frigid fingers, pumped up the pressure and then grubbed a match crookedly against the matchbox, Jack London-style. The match caught, and, shivering, he shoved it up through the baffling and into the glass globe, where the tiny tapered flame found the serpent-hiss of compressed gas and blossomed into a magnificent burst of light that captured and encompassed immediately the cast of all of our work, the scene of ruination that surrounded us: the swamp, where before there had been no swamp. And although it cheered us to have light in which to work, there was an awkward period of transition in which we had to accustom ourselves to the psychology of the new reality, and in this, despite our efforts at sunny optimism, we were not initially successful, erring at first on the side of despair.

The lantern's throw of bright light possessed a peculiar trajectory, fading quickly from an incandescent whiteness that was almost spiritual in quality to a softer and more mellow tone of yellow and then gold before finally, at its farthest reaches, dissolving into fairy dust–like pixels of barely illuminated drizzle. And because it was at these farthest reaches—not so far away, really—that our work extended, it gave us the perception that the entire world was a swamp—that for all our eyes told us, it might as well stretch to the horizon—and we were disoriented, even dispirited, but in the end, there was nothing to do anyway but dig, and so we recovered our hope or faith, if not optimism, and resumed the sledge.

The rain appeared to be lessening, or becoming finer, as the temperature dropped—sleet now, with our hair plastered to our skulls and water running down the backs of our necks, there was nowhere on us that was not soaked, so that we paused from time to time to stand briefly before the lantern, steaming as if burning, to milk a moment of warmth—and our fear now was that the mud might freeze to sludge, and then harden further overnight, like concrete, if we did not get the truck out; though how we were going to do that, with our shovels and sticks and twigs and stones puny compared to the Herculean task before us, we did not know.

I noticed a few stars appearing beyond the outer edges of the lantern's light, felt a stirring of breeze, and in that subtle shifting a sound came to us now, the long baleful mourning of Colter-left-alone, Colter hungry and lonely: a sound so eerily and beautifully like the howl of a wolf that it could not help but ring and resonate, there in the darkness, around our campfire-like focus of the one lantern, within all the mind's chambers of the not-so-distant past. Though our bogged-down truck was not a fallen mastodon in need of rendering, it was still a significant task before us, as our progenitors had always had tasks before them, and as Colter continued to bay and howl, it seemed very much to me that we had gone back in time or that time had moved forward and seized us, for whatever reasons, and carried us backward.

We labored on, wallowing in the frigid trough of our own making, splashing back and forth with stones and branches. I thought briefly of the elegant parties that were probably beginning around this time, down in Houston, and in Austin and Dallas, in Fort Worth and San Antonio. The women in their long glittering dresses, and the men in crisp dark suits, and all the partygoers so clean-scrubbed and tailored.

I wondered how the night's scene must appear to Nathan and was reminded of Van Gogh's painting, *The Road Menders*, one of the first paintings he made after an incarceration at a mental hospital in Arles, in the south of France—indeed, he painted it while still in his upstairs hospital room. The painting exudes the casual grace of the laborers' physical industry and radiates a health that surely the recovering Van Gogh himself was experiencing there in the return of spring. Even the trees seem animated in the painting, and throughout there are the cool pale emerald colors of new spring, of recovery, and of vibrant hope and health and beauty, personified as well in the schematic, rectilinear step-by-step laying-down of stones into the roadbed, so that from the vantage of that upstairs window, with the warm shaded light falling over the village, it must have seemed to Van Gogh like nothing less than an avenue, a path, to salvation.

In my own labors, I glanced up to see if Nathan might have returned to the window to stare down at our work, but saw instead—with some relief—that there was only the continued blue flicker of the Ninja turtles and that the continued evidence of our futility lay for the time being obscured from his consideration.

I wondered what he would make of the evening, after it was over—I knew this logically, if not emotionally; it *would* someday be over—and I daydreamed, as I worked, of my own childhood, embedded in this same landscape. I recovered memories of the five of us—my father, mother, two brothers, and myself—driving up here in the spring to look at the bluebonnets; of riding around in the open-topped jeep on a weekend, smelling this wilder, more fragrant, living country, after a week, or a life, in the city; and of my brothers and I harassing the natives—leaping from the jeep to pursue fruitlessly a roadrunner or jackrabbit, or even one of the newer immigrants, an armadillo. How curious is the nature of the blood that exists in a boy, with regard to these things—and while I am sure that boys are wonderful, rare is the week even now, many years later, in which I do not think and imagine, with the weight of bittersweetness, how much my mother would have loved, as I do, knowing my daughters: watching them grow up, attending their functions, and being a grandmother to them.

We shoveled on, laboring in the freezing mixture. We knew better than to attempt our escape, our exit, prematurely—to make a few short yards, but to then slide off our underwater road and back into the muck, deeper into the muck, would be to fail spectacularly, wasting all of our previous work, and consigning our stones and branches irretrievably deeper into the muck—and so, like the road menders, we continued on, getting everything just right: plotting and planning and scheming.

It stopped raining altogether and grew colder still: wretchedly cold, though deeply beautiful, with the stars seeming to leap into the new blackness, blazing gold. It kept getting colder and colder, until I could not remember being so cold, not even in Montana. The light from the lantern began to dim, and the blue light from within the truck's cab clicked off as Nathan curled up in the back, beneath a mound of sleeping bags, to go to sleep. Colter had stopped howling, so that it was very quiet. The only sounds were those of us sloshing around in the trenches, thigh-deep in places.

Our little underwater road was finally beginning to feel substantial, to feel possible. Lost now more in the process than in any dreamed-of or hoped-for outcome, we continued to scrounge flat stones and cedar-slats. We could walk on our little road, could feel it finally firm beneath our feet, even in the deepest of water, and dikes of slurry rose just as high above us on either side of our proposed trail home. And gradually, constructed at about a ten-degree incline, our little road—a plaza of stone and juniper—emerged from the swamp, and continued then across the surface and through the woods, like the charming boulevard in some charming country other than our own.

The stone path, the mended road, continued on in this manner a good distance out toward the sodden but firm gravel road. It was too far to lay stones and branches all the way there, but our hope was that if we could ever get the truck up out of the wallow-pit, we might be able to gather enough speed to skitter across that last distance, making it all the way to the road, where the firmness, the durability, of the road beneath us would be as great and joyous a success, as tangible a victory as we might ever hope to know. It seemed outlandish to dare to even imagine, much less wish, for such deliverance, and yet viewing our day's work, it seemed possible, and closer than we realized.

I climbed—slithered was more like it—into the truck. Randy would push from behind, then would stand on the bumper and try to rock the springs up and down, to help the tires find traction.

From his nest in the back, Nathan roused sleepily when I started the truck and dropped it into gear. I could feel faintly Randy hopping around on the back like a monkey, or like a frail jockey urging some thunderous warhorse home—his weight made somehow even punier and lonelier by the vastness of discrepancy between ability and desire, though still he continued to hop up and down, as if trying to kick-start the world's largest motorcycle.

I gripped the steering wheel and mashed on the gas, expecting only the heartsick whine and grease-slick spin of nothingness, but right from the very start, it was as if the truck seemed determined to climb up from out of the mud's and the land's grip. From the very beginning, I could feel the tires engaging with stone and wood, could hear and feel the cascade of rocks and branches thudding and clattering beneath us as the spinning wheels sorted and scrabbled through them—the tiny monkey in the back hopping wilder and faster now—and unbelievably, then, with the accelerator still shoved flat, we were slogging up and out of the pit, grinding our howling way forward, born back into the glory of movement, surging and slithering cattywampus along the general direction of the new road beneath us, threading our way perfectly between the twin landscapes of hope and despair, joy and terror.

The fear that we would slide off our narrow path, or that our progress might slow, causing us to bog down once more, was counterbalanced exactly by the flames of hope that, *yes*, this was reality, that despite our fears, we were still moving forward, and the world was scrolling past: oak trees, prickly pear cactus, agarita, juniper, hackberry, hickory.

And then like the evolution of joy, or like the conception, gestation, and delivery of something, the truck was out of danger, was driving as a truck should, skittering over the logs and branches just the way we'd hoped, just the way we'd planned and designed.

It was obvious to us now that as long as we stayed straight and true, we would make it—the branches were snapping and thwapping against the sides of the hurtling truck, like the beatings and croppings of some sturdier jockey spurring us on—and now so certain was our success that Randy had leapt off the back bumper and was running alongside us with a wild whooping cry, leaping for joy with outstretched *pliés* and *tour j'etés* that looked all the more ridiculous for his mud-caked boots and camouflage clothing. He reached the road at the same time that we did, and for me it was the strangest feeling to cruise to a stop on the safety of that hard-packed gravel, secure in the knowledge, no longer taken for granted, that the truck, once it stopped moving, would not begin sinking once more.

The ground was firm beneath us, and it seemed a miracle. It was almost as if we had to start over with the belief, the understanding, of such things.

NEVER WAS THE LUXURY of a hot shower so well received. The hot water melted the ice-slab I had become, returned the fragile heat of life to my body, and perhaps most miraculously of all—in the way that moving water can do—seemed to distance us in time, disproportionately so, from the not-so-long-ago rigor of the excavation, which already seemed a thing of the past, epic and mythic.

We fired up the grill and poured stiff vodka-and-tonics and squeezed a lime into them. We sloshed gas on the pile of campfire wood and somehow got a bonfire going and sat on the porch as the steaks grilled and the potatoes baked. We looked out at the frozen stars and relived the adventure. There was still every bit as huge a vacancy in me as that which the truck had left behind—a bottomlessness, is what it felt like, and a fragility, but it felt good to have the truck safely in the barn garage, rather than still half-sunk out in the frozen wilderness, and good also to be with Randy and Nathan, and watching the fire: watching the sparks pop and float up toward the stars.

The wind had shifted again, turning even harder out of the north, and was dryer. Colter lay beside me, the fire reflecting in his dark eyes, groaning and almost purring as I petted him from time to time, with the world ahead of us, and the territory of the unknown, seeming strangely larger than it had ever been: seeming almost precisely as large as the sky and space visible in the night beyond us and in the eternity of days that would follow, were sure to follow, from this point forward, not just in our own short mortal days, but in all the days of the turning of the world-to-come.

It was impossible, I think, to feel any more insignificant against such a backdrop, and yet what a paradox that was, for how could such insignificance and tininess be the vessel, the reservoir, for such immensity of heartache, and for such fierce wonder?

THAT NIGHT AN ICE SHIELD fell over the world, so that when I awakened on the first of January the curve of the hills and the fields and woods were all encased in starlit ice, the land's dark reflection burning as if from some interior fire.

Nathan and Randy were sleeping in. I dressed and fixed a cup of coffee, acutely conscious of the almost mechanical advancement of time—or rather, my perception of it as thus, on this one day—and certainly, if I could have hesitated, or even gone back in time—if I could do anything to keep from going into the new year without my mother, I would have turned back, would have lingered, would have sought whatever quiet eddy there might have been, where things could continue being as they had been.

There was just enough trace of stiffness from the labors of the day before to feel good: not a true soreness, but a reminder that I had done something. The frozen gravel crunched underfoot, and the frosty air penetrated so deep when I inhaled that it seemed somehow that I might be breathing starlight: that such a thing might be possible, there in that brief and fast-dying blink of time between darkness and dawn.

The place I was going was a place I had never hunted before. During the November hunt, in a shady tangle of oak and juniper growing on a sandy flat at the juncture of a steep tributary, a narrow slot canyon down which immense granite boulders had tumbled, I had spied a torn-up sapling, so freshly scraped that the sap was still oozing from it, and the slivers and tendrils of bark that had fallen to the ground were still so bright and unoxidized as to seem still living; as if, were one to place them back upon the abraded bark of the sapling, they might yet graft and grow.

My plan was to nestle into the boulders of that crevice and to watch the sandy trail that wound through those trees along the creek, and to see if the buck that had rubbed that tree with his antlers in November, marking his territory, might wander by. I had brought a set of antlers with which to rattle, to simulate the sound of two other bucks sparring in his territory, and a grunt tube, with which to make the deep low calls of another deer.

Although I had walked every inch of these thousand acres in the darkness any number of times, both with and without a flashlight, I had never navigated my way across this landscape, nor any other that I could remember, with the world so perfectly encased in ice.

Every branch, every limb, every blade of winter-dead grass was encased in a thick chrysalis of ice, which slid heavy and away from me as I passed through the brush, and which bobbed, clacking, in my wake. The world underfoot was likewise coated with a shell of illuminated ice, and even if I had not known that it would not last, even if I had believed that this was the newer and more frightening world-to-come—that from here on out, all would be ice—I think that I still would have found it beautiful.

I crossed over the creek, which I had been able to hear roaring even from a distance: an exciting sound, so different from the usual quiet trickle, the riffling gurgle of memory. The usually clear creek was now the color of chocolate milk, and frothy with foam and roiling waves, spread wide beyond its usual perimeters. The severed branches and limbs of oaks and willows cascaded down its center, and smaller branches bobbed and wheeled crazily into the choppy eddies as if seeking an escape, and I had to pick my crossing carefully, working from memory as to where the pitch was widest, and where the little creek, once able to be jumped across and would be one day—soon—again, was narrowest.

Darkness, ice, flood: I had never seen such a world before, yet it made perfect sense to me. I inhabited it gracefully, like a guest arriving right on time. The high wind above continued to scrub the stars bright and burnished, and I made my way over the slippery ice hills to the secret cleft from which I would hunt that morning and settled in out of the wind, pulled on another coat for warmth, and then was motionless, as if having been claimed by the landscape, absorbed like nothing more than so much of the night-before's rain.

I could hear the creek below me, still roaring and charging: the perfect shadow, perfect systolic pulse from the steady torrents of the day before, which had spent all night charging down every other hill and every other creek in order to arrive at this creek, this one place, at this one point in time, and then carrying on past.

Yesterday's flood, arriving today—late, and yet on time—from other places I knew, a weaving of names that would mean nothing, or next-to-nothing, to those who did not know those places or names, but that meant the world to me: White Oak Creek, Buffalo Creek, Willow Creek, Coal Creek.

By afternoon, these same charging waters—the ones I could hear but not see—would be nearer to San Antonio; by the next evening, or the following morning, to the estuaries of the Gulf, and then amongst the silt- and sand-colored waves of ocean surf.

In the pre-dawn darkness I found a hiding place beneath an older, larger juniper that was growing between the symmetrical halves of a frost-split granite boulder, each boulder-half the size of an upright refrigerator, and I settled in to wait for daylight and to watch the canyon and the sandy little grove of oak and juniper below. I thought about nothing, merely waited.

An hour, two hours, melted as if but a second, though not the ice. I didn't move. It felt good to remain so still, so motionless, lulled by the cold blue wind from the north and by the sound of the water, the quick flood.

There were no clouds. The rising sun touched the tips of the bright winter-green junipers on the rim of the other side of the canyon first and then began painting slowly but steadily with its yellow winterlight the vegetation and boulders beneath that rim, the light descending into the canyon, brush stroke by brush stroke, and onto my camouflaged hiding spot: though still the ice-shell held, so that the ice-casts of all things burned now not with starlight but with the fractal radiance of diamonds and rainbows.

I sat entranced, almost as if not daring, or as if forgetting, to breathe, until finally I felt a faint stirring of warmth on my face, the winter sun finally beginning to catch, and the dazzle began to loosen from the hills, the prismatic colors sliding and slipping away from all that was cloaked with the once-shining ice. The sparkle vanished, yet in its place, the vibrant colors of the native landscape and native vegetation were revealed as if born again, fresh-scrubbed and bright.

Still I waited, almost perfectly motionless, and was content to do so: listening, watching, waiting. Every half hour, I would blow quietly on the grunt tube or click the drybone antlers together lightly, rattling their tines against one another. Those sounds would be lost beneath the blue sky, but I did not despair, I had all day, and I rested there between the cleaved rocks and watched the canyon before me and continued to rest or reside in that space where hours were confused with moments.

When the buck came in to his grove, he was moving quickly, almost at a trot. His body, light brown, was pale and clean, as if washed by the rain. He was a large deer with large antlers that were surprisingly pale—almost sun-bleached—and as he hurried down the canyon, passing me on my right side, only twenty yards away, I saw that his black hooves were shiny, as if newly polished, and the late morning sun caught his eyes so that they gleamed.

I lifted the rifle quickly but carefully—he paused, detecting that movement between him and the sun—and finding the seam behind his shoulder at the top of the heart, I fired.

He leapt hump-backed, stumbled, and then galloped down the trail he'd been on, as if merely in more of a hurry now to reach that grove of trees, and though I felt confident he was mortally wounded, that he would run but a few more bounds and then collapse, heartshot, I knew better than to jump up and follow, which might cause him to draft one final surge of adrenaline, giving him the strength to carry him far beyond my ken or reach.

I continued waiting, and only now began to daydream, and to think about the conscious world, the real world of the present: of the fact that it was New Year's Day and that I had just hunted and shot, and was about to gather, a fine deer. I wondered if Randy and Nathan were back in camp, or if they were out hunting in the bright cool sun. I listened to the rush of the briefly wide creek below, admired the sun-painted cliffs and rocks on the other side of the canyon a little longer, and then rose, stretching my legs, and walked over to where the deer had been standing when I'd shot, where I found, as I'd known I would, a scatter of hair and some drops of bright red blood, still shining wet upon the granite and in the pinkened gravel of the game trail.

For how many tens of thousands of years have hunters known such a mix of feelings—the satisfaction of success mixed with the fuller evidence of the responsibility inherent in the taking of any food from the earth, whether planted crop or harvested wild? The weight of our own existence, made so startlingly manifest; the going-on.

I followed the drops of blood straight down the trail, walking carefully, and I remained confident that the body of the deer would be just a little farther on, around the next bend—in the cool of that little grove, perhaps, pitched down into the sand.

In the grove, there was less blood, but the trail was still evident. The deer was taking longer leaps, the leaves were stirred up from each track, and now and again I found another loosened hair, another Rorschach of bright red blood cradled in the brown grasp of an upturned leaf.

I followed the trail out of the trees and across the sand and back onto the puddled stone of slickrock that pitched down toward the wide-rushing rain-swollen creek. There was a little ledge spanning the creek just a few yards upstream, a ledge across which I could usually walk, but that was covered now with the wide rush of the flood, and over which cascaded the sheet of a little waterfall.

I bent and studied the blood sign. The drops led straight to the creek. I looked across the creek to the other side—too far for me to leap, but not for a deer—and saw the stippling of tracks from where deer regularly leapt this crossing. I did not see the brown body of the deer lying down, pitched over onto its side. I did not see the great nest of antlers cradled in the grass just a short distance ahead, visible above even the winter-dead remains of grass and brush, the sight that usually greets the successful hunter.

Walking carefully, and starting to feel the first inklings of concern and doubt, I went upstream to the crossing place and made my way carefully across the flatrock ledge, the broad roiling sheet of water shuddering against my ankles, not quite over the tops of my boots, the water so silt-clouded from the flood that I could not see the stone beneath me.

I reached the other side and hurried over to the spot where the deer's leap would have carried him—the spot where all those other tracks were stippled, like the prints of long-jumpers in a sand pit—and being careful not to disturb any, I set my rifle against a tree and got down on my hands and knees in the storm-wet grass and began parsing among the tracks, hoping for the surest indicator, the brilliance of blood, and, failing that, another piece of hair—possibly this deer's, possibly not—and, failing that, a divot of earth so freshly torn that the individual sand grains were still glistening: a line, then, a cast of direction to set off into, in my blindness.

I didn't see how the shot could be anything other than precise at that distance, but if my aim had somehow floated a few inches, penetrating the lungs but not touching the heart, then the deer—particularly a big muscular deer like this one—could in theory run for hours, on-again and off-again, before bedding down somewhere miles away beneath a tree, or in a nest of brush, remaining vigilant, even if incapacitated, for days.

That is not the nature of what deer do when they are hurt badly, however. Their nature when mortally wounded is to return immediately and directly to the core of their home, stop and hunker down, and wait to heal.

I did not think this deer was hit in the lungs, though, nor in any other lesser place. I felt certain this deer had been struck in the heart, and even as I continued searching on my hands and knees for the most microscopic of clues, I kept glancing up into the meadow, believing that I was simply overlooking the body, as often happens: the hundred and fifty pounds of deer somehow suddenly vanishing, lying down instead of standing, and lifeless rather than alive. Everything disappearing almost immediately back into the protective coloration of the deer's native home, back into the time-crafted perfect camouflage of native vegetation: everything except the crown of ant-lers, which, when upright, blend perfectly with the branches of the forest, but which, when pitched sideways in the middle of a field, appear as incon-gruous as the detached harrow for a farmer's tractor. What was once hidden gracefully, meshed into the safety of the natural world, the human eye is drawn to, and quickly. As if all can find death immediately, while the task of finding life remains so much more challenging.

I SPENT THE REST OF THE DAY TRACKING, often on my hands and knees, or in a bent stoop, moving slowly: following one unraveling radial of tracks after another, as far into the forest as I could, before that skein vanished, or became entangled with another. I panicked that I would lose this deer—that I *had* lost it—and then I despaired. To lose any deer, or any animal, but especially a great one, is one of the sourest feelings a hunter can know, rearranging and nearly invalidating what is already a complex and highly evolved moral negotiation in the short realm between life and death. Often the hunter feels like weeping, or is paralyzed with grief when such a misfor-tune occurs, and may quit hunting for a year, or other times altogether.

I had no way of knowing if the tracks and trails I followed were those that my deer had taken or those of dozens of others. Over on the back side of the deer pasture, up and over the top of Buck Hill, nearly a mile from where I had shot, I found a drop of fresh blood on a rock, and, believing it to be from my deer—for no one else had fired a shot—I worked that area hard, hoping to find the deer bedded down under a tree, waiting to die, or dead. There were no other clues that I could find, out on the rocks like that, to indicate in which direction the animal had been traveling, or the nature of the wound, or even if the blood was that of a deer.

I searched until dark, casting in wider and wider circles around that one mysterious drop of blood, with each deerless hour that passed reducing pro-portionately the already faint hope that I would find this deer.

I had examined and re-examined every square inch of the back side: I was convinced there was no dead deer back there. It occurred to me, with the slimmest of hopes, that this blood drop had nothing to do with my deer and that perhaps I had simply overlooked my deer there at the creek. I hiked back that long mile to where I had shot the deer and played it all over again: followed the initial heavy blood sign right down to the creek, then crossed on that ledge, and examined the other side, where still I could find nothing.

I went back to the blood side yet again and this time went up and down the stream, searching, wondering if the deer might have stopped at the wild creek, panicked by its injury and by the creek's unfamiliar, flood-swollen state, and veered left or right, but here, too, I could discern no tracks, blood, or hair.

There was still a little bit of light left in the day. I decided to go back to camp and see if Randy and Nathan were in, to get them to help me search, and to bring Colter along on a leash to see if he, with his incredible bird-finding nose, might be inspired to investigate the area in such a way as to give me a hint whether the deer had turned and run along the creek bank upstream or downstream. Indeed, it was my hope that if the deer was piled up somewhere nearby, dead under a juniper bush, Colter might point this out to me, that he might pull me over in that direction, tugging on his leash, urging me to investigate an area I had bypassed.

Randy and Nathan were gone when I got back to camp, so I made a quick sandwich, left a note, got Colter, and headed back out. I'd been walking all day, slowly but ceaselessly, and was tired. I had also been feeling uncomfortable back in camp, separated from the deer like that, or separated from the search.

I took Colter directly to the canyon, where the blood had dried from red to brown. Already it looked like something ancient, even geologic, rather than the legacy of anything that had happened mere hours ago.

Colter dropped his nose to the spot anyway, suddenly electric with interest, and holding his leash, I puzzled over how sage he seemed in that moment: as if, in that single scent, he was able to delve into and discern that which had happened in the past, as well as casting ahead to the future, and the knowledge not only of where that deer had been, but also of where it might yet be.

Stub tail twitching, he followed the trail quickly down to the creek, then snuffled hurriedly left and right. Whether he was nosing out my earlier scent from where I had tracked up and down the creek or was still detecting the deer's scent, I had no real way of knowing, although I was grateful for his enthusiasm.

As I had done, he hurried across the creek on the rock ledge—the water had already dropped several inches, so that the stone was dimly visible, though the water was still fast and turbulent and crawfish-colored—and hot on the trail now, with me hurrying along behind, still gripping the leash, he ran a few more steps, heading toward the tracked-up sandpit, where I had anticipated the deer to land, but then Colter stopped, slamming on the brakes so hard that I tripped over him.

So suddenly did he halt, and so confused did he seem, that I thought he might have gotten wind of a sluggish January water moccasin. And like a snake charmer himself, he lifted his broad head and stared back upwind, across to the other side of the creek, across the plunge-pool that sat relatively serene below the little waterfall.

With his muscles beginning to quiver and tense, he lifted one paw, cautious at first—as if he was receiving a contradiction of the senses, as if he could not quite believe that which the natural world was telling him—but then, increasingly confident, he tucked that left paw all the way tight against his chest and crouched, striking the beautiful pose of dog-on-point.

I stood there puzzled for several seconds, wondering if he was only just now picking up the blood-scent that I thought I had already shown to him. This wasn't what I wanted at all, and carefully, I tugged on his leash, hoping to entice him into walking farther downstream.

He was staunch, however, and would not release to my tug. His green eyes bulged and burned with an odd mix of confusion and certainty, and I knelt to pat him on his chest, and to thank him for his intensity if not his accuracy, and to urge him along. There was so little time left in the day.

It was only then, down at eye level with him, that I saw the world from his perspective, and saw the deer's antlers sticking up from the center of the mudwater pond below the falls, with only the very candelabra tips sticking up: five or six of the very tip-tops of the longer tines, only an inch or two above water, so that at first glance, or no-glance, they would have appeared like the tips of a big tree limb that had been washed downstream.

Colter eased his nose forward. The antler-branches were almost close enough to reach out and touch. And though I was looking right at them, and recognized them now as the top inch-tips of antlers, I could not yet reconcile the transition, in my mind, of how the entire body of a huge deer could be reduced now to but an inch, or two inches, of bone. The antlers themselves were almost the same color as the medium in which they now resided.

Still gripping Colter's leash, I eased forward, squinting, and now—as much by faith or hope at first, as by true visual acuity—I could see dimly the outline of the submerged deer, with the deer's underwater silhouette still almost as much a function of imagination as reality, and the deer's coat almost the exact color of brown as the night-before's floodwaters.

I thanked Colter and gave general thanks to the deer and to the world, too—I had definitely not found this deer; it had found me, had been *delivered* to me—and I reached out and gripped the underwater antlers and pulled the deer to shore, dragged it up onto the grass on the other side of the creek, not thirty yards from where I had shot. It was a huge deer, as large a deer as I had ever killed on the deer pasture, and Colter released himself from his point and began sniffing at the deer, checking it out, running all around it and nosing it, as if surprised and agitated at this strange revelation that he, even with all his millennial innate wisdom, had never previously understood—that creatures like deer, and, who knew now, perhaps even quail and doves and pheasants, might be found beneath us, in some other, lower world's layer.

I petted him, congratulated him, and sat there in the dusk with our discovery, our little miracle, there in the bluing of twilight, on that cold clear first day of January.

It was a marvel and an amazement to me that a thing I had so desired could be given to me, returned to me, in such dramatic and miraculous fashion, even as the heavier and colder knowledge returned to me all over again that there were other things, much more desired, that would never be forthcoming: that I would have to be forever-after content with memories, thoughts, and recollections, and those strange quiet moments of communion when the two worlds, the departed and the still-here, yet occasionally intersect and transact, as if between the thin layers of some larger world, or two worlds, above and beneath the surface.

I still felt alone, there above the surface, though it was a beautiful surface, the one she had brought me out into—and, grateful for that, despite my sorrow, I hauled the deer up into the woods and cleaned it, as the men in our family had always hunted deer back when she had still been living, and then I started back to camp in darkness, with Colter trotting alongside me, and my rifle in one hand, and dragging the heavy deer behind.

AOUDADS

SIX DAYS PASS FAST when you're building a myth—or living in one, sinking ever deeper in the years of accretion. Even if each accruing year brings only one or two new stories, then over the course of a lifetime, or half a lifetime, an incredible architecture can and will be constructed nonetheless, an architecture of family and self, of place and time, and even consequence and meaning.

Even the dramatically incorrect mistakes are preserved and put to good use in the erection of such an edifice, and the good or lucky or even just plain interesting events are highlighted and revered brightest of all. I'm not sure what the cultural or evolutionary advantage of such internal, personal architecture is, but I suspect that it is something as complex and wonderful and ultimately valuable—perhaps even necessary—as the construction of the intricate mazes of honeycombs in bee colonies or the underground multi-chambered warrens of prairie dogs. And I sometimes wonder if the Biblical descriptions of the gold-lined streets of heaven, and the ornate mansions with all those many rooms, are both allegory and reality and that there are times when we are already living in the midst of such treasures, certainly not through any earned efforts, but glimpsing such dwellings anyway—and that the many rooms in the father's mansion are but the stories—the useful stories of love, compassion, and courage, and even sheer undeserving luck that we're able to lay in during the mortal years, each of us accumulating such stories—bright myths—for the afterlife, as a stonemason might hoard the finest self-selected, hand-picked stones for the one great creation of his life, the dwelling place in which he will spend all of his afterlife.

I might be wrong. There might be no connection at all between heaven and earth. And the world and its great religions might all be completely literal, as fundamental and nonnegotiable in the long run as the tangible blocks of stones that I am trying to make abstract, vaporous things of spirit and memory rather than the dense-packed residue of the ages: silica, carbon, feldspar, iron, potassium, phosphorous. Pyrite.

AT THE DEER PASTURE, it seems to me sometimes that it is not so much that we have constructed our own little myths and legends over the years, or constructed any certain edifice, but that instead have wandered into a mythological dwelling place that was already made, replete with all the many chambers and rooms and caverns of creek and canyon ridge and ravine, hollow and swale, syncline and anticline, trough and depression, knob and peak. That the architecture was made long ago and has always been waiting, and that to claim it, we have only to learn how to fit it—indeed, how to revere and worship it, as well as the stunning force that made it.

And yet, within those chambers, and out and about on these thousand acres (and from that lodestone, on out into the rest of our lives), we continue to make, or observe, our own little myths. Perhaps these smaller constructs even mimic, in some fashion, the larger arrangement of the ages before us. Perhaps, if we are allowed to consider the richness of metaphor and allegory, that might even be one of the lessons that some larger force, for whatever reason—call it love, or compassion—desired, and desires, to impress upon us.

In any event, I have noticed here a proclivity for storytelling, mythmaking, tale-building. The affinity is in us for some reason, was instilled there for some purpose, and again, it has to me the same pleasant, comforting feeling as hefting a nice big square-cut stone, dense and durable—and our mortal lives, are the quarry from which the stones derive.

I'M NOT SURE WHEN I heard some of the stories the second time or, certainly, the hundredth. Nor can I quite trace, in the looking-back, the continuum between the joy of hearing one of the stories for the first time, with the imagination of the first-time listener fully engaged, and the feeling of pride of familiarity, then, upon hearing one of the stories of place for the fifth or sixth time—my cousins and brothers and I knowing it so well by that point that we could fill in any of the gaps or skips and could anticipate each forthcoming image, if not quite yet knowing precisely each telling's choice of language or cadence.

I would have guessed the continuum would have ended there and that our task as children, even grown children, was to continue listening to the old stories, which, in their hundredth-or-more telling, were now more of a comfort to the tellers than to the listeners: the tellers resurrecting memories so vibrant that they would never vanish, never be buried or plowed asunder. The tellers reassuring themselves of this fact with each telling.

I would not have been able to foresee that across that continuum there might be another phase, as the stories took root in us and became somehow our responsibilities, as listeners, even though we had never lived those stories.

Having heard the stories on each and every hunt—sometimes at lunch, sometimes in the evenings—certainly, we possess the ability, if not the authority, to tell them almost as well as the tellers. To tell them well enough to keep them alive—though in our own second-telling, there will surely be somewhat the absence of the strange shine or luster that accompanied the original tellers' tellings, as they polished bright once more their memories.

Our own second-tellings will be polishing only the memories of memories, and will be like shadows, rather than the things themselves.

But somewhere, it occurred to us that that would be required of us one day—that we would be in charge of deciding which stories to keep alive, in telling, and which ones would vanish with the men who had once told them.

Someday, we would be required to cull and select, to weed and prune, to caretake in some strange fashion, the memory of those who could no longer remember.

Do we keep the story about the night the wild pigs chased Uncle Jimmy up a tree, even though we were not there—were still nearly twenty years away from being there with the river of time already sweeping past that spot? Yes, certainly. But what about the time their friend, Newt, who sometimes hunted with them in those early years, caught all the baby pigs with his belt, made into a lasso, and stored them in a little dollhouse of a corral, on a cliff way back in the middle of nowhere, so that for a day or so, his fellow hunters were puzzled by the little grunts and squeals, until they discovered his "pigpen"—a crude structure that still stands, weathered and rotting, the pigpen itself more shadow of story, forty years later?

Yes. But others tumble, disintegrate, are washed away.

There is this one spot, this one tilted rock along a trail, where, my father informs me every time we pass, he killed a deer when he was a young man: fired a long shot with his open-sight 30–30 from up on that cliff, nearly two hundred yards distant. He points to it. The cedar has grown in over what was once open country, so that it's hard to imagine being able to see so far.

The deer fell instantly and lay kicking, briefly, just as his father came walking around the corner, so that it was almost as if the buck had landed in his lap. My grandfather had not been hunting that deer, had not even known it was on the trail such a short distance in front of him—but here it was now suddenly, as if having fallen from the sky.

Every time we pass that place, my father tells me that story, so that it is almost—*almost*—mine, and I am never able to pass that stone (the blood has long since been washed clean) without remembering that telling and that image, so that now the landscape is an intermediary in the story.

The landscape initiated the original story, and now it acts as the liaison between the teller and the listener—as close a conduit to memory as is perhaps possible, closer even than the written word, or the recorded word—for to stand next to that rock in the autumn, and to look up at that cliff from which the shot was fired, is quite a different thing from reading about it or looking at a photograph of it, and in some comforting and positive way deflects back toward the source, the story: though still, it is an echo, and the main river, the one river of each person's life, is moving past, is long past.

SO THE OLD GUYS have a lifetime of stories, which serve as their own foundation, as well as in some immeasurable and unknowable way our own foundation—my cousins' and brothers' and mine. As the old guys themselves, Dad, Uncle Jimmy, and gone-away Granddad—composed of stories—serve, of course, as our foundation, too, in a tangible, measurable, knowable way. Excuse me for belaboring the obvious then, but while it's certain we'd be here without the old-timers' stories, it's far less certain that we'd have any foundation, without their stories, even if for us they are echoes of stories.

We would go on to witness and experience our own stories, surely, with or without that foundation of the past, but in our hands, then, our own stories would be like loose rubble: fine quarrystone, perhaps, but without the foundation of the old stories against which to compare and contrast, and replicate or alter, our own stacked stories would possess less structure—and in that formlessness, I suspect, less power and meaning.

So it's important, I understand, to not get up and leave the room when my father—Grandpa Charlie, the kids are calling him now, a moniker that would once have seemed so alien to me, but that now sounds right, and natural—begins one of the old stories as if for the thousandth time. He knows we've all heard it before—often he'll be telling it to Uncle Jimmy, who likely as not experienced the story with him, fifty or sixty years ago.

It's important, I realize, for me to hang in there and hear it again, for that thousandth time, listening to the story this time as one would listen to the rain falling on the tin roof, or to the clinking sound of stones being stacked outside on some ongoing masonry project, two upon one, one upon two— like overlaying unlike, unlike overlaying like, so that even in the stories' differences, the wall being constructed is pleasing in its uniformity, and strong, and imminently durable.

NOTHING MUCH HAPPENED to me on this year's hunt. As the land ties us together, linking us and our stories to our elder relatives and their stories, so too does our quarry. And yet as we age, the chemical within us that once made us want so badly to shoot a deer or turkey has waned considerably.

Uncle Jimmy and Dad still go out into the hills, carrying a rifle, as if waiting for the inspiration, the need, the desire, to return—like a retired farmer going out and looking up at the sky for rain, is how I think of it, even though the farmer no longer has any crops planted—*habit*—but the urge never returns, for they observe the deer, watch antlered bucks slipping through the cedar, but never fire any more.

Perhaps we imagine that it, the missing desire, is like the deer used to be, and it is that desire we are searching for, rather than deer, when we go out on their walks, still carrying a rifle.

I notice it in myself more each year. More and more, I do not shoot deer that in the old days I would have shot. I have killed dozens of deer, but now it seems as if they are almost all slipping away from me, escaping like sand through my outstretched fingers, flowing away, and I do not mind. I too am content only to wander the hills with my rifle in hand—Old Granddad's ancient .270, rebored after the First World War—and to walk quietly, and take in the world's scent, and to listen, and to just see what happens.

IT RAINED LIKE STINK THIS YEAR: not the frequent hill country fog and mist, nor one of the brief yet powerful thunderstorms that accompany cold fronts from the north smashing into the humid southeast Gulf weather systems, but instead, a cold and steady toadstrangler, for day upon day and night upon night.

Still, we had come to hunt, and so on opening morning we each departed for our favorite places, our nooks and niches, where we might or might not be able to stay dry. Curious to see what the land would bring us, this year. Seven of us, this year. (Frank was sick in Vermont, stomach virus and high fever, unable to travel; a disappointment to us all, and a feeling as unsettling to me as if the stone wall were to have one of its middle emplacements pulled out.)

Nothing happened, all that first morning. No one shot any deer, no one saw any deer. I sat for hours in my camouflage rainsuit beneath a big oak, rain dripping hypnotically onto my head and shoulders, lulling me into a motionless trance. I waited and waited, believing as a hunter believes that at any moment, a nice buck was going to come walking past.

The only thing remotely like that occurred just before I was about to stand up and stretch and walk squish-booty back to camp for lunch. A thoroughly drenched raccoon (we were to see several, that year) came trundling through the tall grass, head down and rump tipped in that car-up-on-jacks way the big ones have of walking.

He was heading straight for me, heading straight for my tree, and it was easy to see that he had but one idea on his mind, to get out of that miserable rain.

I was perfectly still and perfectly camouflaged. He kept coming on, thirty feet, twenty feet, ten feet—stopping now and again briefly to snuffle at some rich scent, some delicacy beneath the rotting autumn leaves.

Finally he was right at the tip of my boots—I could have nudged him if I wanted—and, not knowing what etiquette demanded—clearing my throat seemed like too human of a thing to do—I instead merely wiggled my toes, which were less than a foot away from him.

He was so cool. He didn't blow up like a ball of dynamite, all heart-stricken and wall-eyed, the way I would have.

Instead, he froze, reared up on his hind legs (his front paws clasped in front of him as if begging my pardon for some ill-considered intrusion), peered at me only briefly, as if to be absolutely certain of what he was seeing, but not looking too long—as if believing that staring, too, would be rude—and seemingly without regret, he dropped back down to all fours and ambled back off into the steady rain.

Nothing else happened all day. And I doubt that I can carry that image, that little story, beyond my own life—it is no one's foundation—but it was a quarrystone in my accretion, and a fine way to spend a rainy morning, and a fine thing to see. And to remember. Handling the image in my memory as if it was a stone, trying to decide which way to stack it.

ON DAY TWO, I almost made a kill. Once again I had sat quietly, watching and waiting, but had seen nothing; and growing chilled and miserable, I rose and began walking, not really hunting but just slogging, moving through the dripping cedar as if in a dream. From time to time I would remember that I was supposed to be hunting and would resume skulking and scouting, paying attention to shadows and wind direction, faint noises near and far—but somehow it was mortally tiring in the steady rain like that, and soon enough I would slip back into the straight-ahead plod, the slog-o-rama.

Until I heard the turkeys, that is. They gobbled only once, sounding very far away, and, though I had never heard turkeys gobble in a driving rain before, they sounded very wet and very unhappy, feeble and dispirited: ass-whipped, dejected with the world. I could see them in my mind's eye, marching single file, feathers sodden, trudging as if on the way back from some country funeral, their once-iridescent shimmering feathers now drooping and rain-blacked.

So familiar am I with the lay of this land that it seemed to me that even from that one little distant outburst of squabble-gobble—one lone gobbler lifting his voice, perhaps, to protest the steady drenching—I was pretty sure where they were.

In my mind, I was exactly sure where they were—I imagined I could see the tree they were marching past, half a mile away—and with all the previous rain-torpor vanished from me immediately, and the full blood of the hunt returned (*this*, perhaps, was the thing I and the older guys had been out wandering in the fields in search of), I galloped through the woods, wet cedar fronds swatting me in the face and knotty oak limbs smacking my forehead as I rushed toward the place where I thought I could best lay in wait to ambush them, if they came wandering my way, taking the path I had assigned to them in my imagination, and that, with every bit of my hunter's fire, hunter's force, I was now trying to will them to take. And all this energy was being dispensed while at the same time I was trying to balance the negative capability of not thinking about them at all in order to reduce the risk of alerting their keen senses to the mere resonance of my being.

I was down in Panther Hollow, also sometimes called Turkey Hollow, near where the fence divides our property from the next: cleaving the creek in two, in places, as the ancient rusting barbed wire and drill-blasted metal fenceposts zigzag back and forth across the meander of the shallow, narrow creek, down in that dark hollow of hickory and oak, where nobody ever goes, and where certainly, if you went across that line, nobody would ever know.

I could hear the turkeys coming right down the fenceline, as I'd hoped they would. I was wearing camo, was hunkered behind a cedar, motionless, and it was raining hard on all of us. Surely with their bedraggled, down-tipped heads, they would not notice me, but would pass right by me, close enough for me to almost reach out and grab one by the neck if I desired.

I didn't move a muscle—I emptied my mind of desire and became the rain itself—but somehow they sensed or saw me, for I heard the first telltale *putt!*, the sound of me being busted, and then a quick scrabbling, followed by a thumpy, screechy, bass cello or guitar sound, as that lead bird hopped nimbly over the fence and detoured onto the other land, traveling away from me now at a ninety-degree angle.

No problem. They had to be walking single-file—the trail through the dense cedar and along that old fence was too narrow for them to do anything but that—and if the lead one scooched away, well, not to worry, I'd take the number two bird, or even number three or four or five. I remained motionless, confident in my hiding spot, and waited.

But once more, I heard the little alarm peep, from not fifteen yards away, just on the other side of a big cedar, followed by that same guitar-twanging sound of a turkey vaulting the fence.

Again, I remained squint-eyed and motionless—they couldn't *possibly* see me—but this time, through the dense screening of cedar, I thought I saw the airborne head of a gobbler, bright blue in the rain, as he fluttered over that low fence like a gymnast mounting the parallel bars, or even taking low preliminary leaps on a trampoline—a little three- or four-foot leap in which he ascended, wings still tucked to his side and legs paddling the air heroically, just enough of a bound to clear that fence—and then descended on the other side, the safe side, and watching the place where I was hiding all the while.

The third turkey vaulted the fence in the same spot, in this same manner, as did the fourth and the fifth. I continued to refuse to believe they were seeing me, even though as each one floated over that top strand of fence, I could see the beady eye of each lone jumper fixed on me with an eerie intensity, scowling stern as a judge.

Maybe the number six bird will be different, I told myself, trying to pretend that with all their fretsome and concurrent gobbling and purring and putting and fussing, they weren't broadcasting the word to each and all, 5'7" *Caucasian male/blue eyes/balding/gap-toothed/kind of lecherous-looking/twelve o'clock sharp, fifteen yards out*; at the same place, the number six bird made his little vault, and I thought, *Maybe number seven will keep on coming on*, but there was no number seven, only absence, after that.

I could see them, scattered here and there, wandering confused and nervous, unsure of what to do next, and trying to regroup: a blue head here, a long beard behind a cedar there, drumstick legs, the scuttling silhouette of a body, a snakelike head peering out from behind an oak tree before *putting*! and ducking back behind the tree.

I could have taken almost any one of them, a fairly simple twenty- or thirty-yard shot, climbed the fence, taken a few strides, lifted the old tom up, and walked back onto my property—no one would ever have known, and hell, maybe even the other turkeys wouldn't have known—but I wasn't even remotely tempted. They had been on our property, but now they had beaten me, fair and square.

In the old days, I would have been tempted sorely, but this day I just sat there in the rain and watched them and smiled at how close it had been, and at the waning of desire, though not pleasure.

And after they had hurried off into the woods, and I rose to leave, I looked down at my soggy boots and saw then what surely each of them had been seeing: the solid band of duct tape, as brilliant as the gleaming aluminum fuselage of an airplane, from where I had repaired my old sole-flapping boots that morning; and I laughed, marveling at how it must have leapt out at them, back there in the dark hollow, shiny as a new beer can on that gloomy day, and at the luck of those turkeys, and how they just weren't meant to be gotten that day.

I was just pleased to have wanted one. To have wanted one pretty badly.

EVENINGS SPENT FIXING big old artery-clogging stroke-summoning steak-and-potato dinners, or jambalaya, or fried ham and red-eye gravy, or fried doves and biscuits and cream gravy. Song of the South: Old Granddaddy underground, Uncle Jimmy still fighting his way back from his stroke, my father and I unscathed for now.

It's not like we eat like this all the time. Maybe just once a year.

Telling stories—that rain still drumming the tin roof—and mixing, now, some of the newer ones—my cousins' and mine—with the braid of some of the really old ones.

Hardly ever are the evening stories about deer. About the only time a deer story gets told is when someone brings a new deer into camp, and we are standing around admiring it, and are reminded of other deer, sometimes from that same locale, other times not, and sometimes appearing similar to the new deer, though other times, different. Memories unfolding upon memories, like dominoes.

NOTHING, THEN. A raccoon by my boot and a flock of turkeys spooked by my boot. Two little things to add like keepsakes into a small bag or pouch, a life.

Day three: more slog-hiking, walking all over the place, trying to burn off some calories from all the heavy feeding. By this time I was not only accustomed to the steady rain, but was also kind of enjoying it. It made everything quiet, and I was kind of getting into the routine of coming back to camp each evening, drenched, and drying my boots by the fire, getting them dry just barely in time to put on the next day, and start all over again. In such inclement weather, there can be a solace and comfort in the repetition of small things.

I went way over onto the back side. Randy had shot a deer on the east side the day before, a nice buck with dark mahogany antlers, and cousin Rick had shot a nice one at dusk that same day. I still didn't have the fire of old desire that's often required to take a deer—as if that desire must reach a certain depth or temperature within the heart of the hunter in order to kindle the hunter's luck—in order for the deer to present itself to the hunter, almost as if summoned—giving the hunter a chance, at least.

I just wasn't to that point. I was enjoying walking around, but I just didn't really want a deer. I don't know why, and I don't know what I would have done if I'd seen one. I was just walking.

I believe completely what hunters the world over have counseled since time immemorial: that to truly have success in catching up with one's quarry unawares, it is best for the hunter to empty the mind of his or her desires, while simultaneously and seemingly paradoxically remaining intensely aware of all the tiny necessary steps required of the hunter's rendezvous—faint sounds, tracks, wind direction, hiding cover, forage, water, escape routes.

So my mind's eye was empty; I was doing everything right, even if I wasn't all excited about happening upon a deer. I was in the perfect state of mind to stumble onto something, and passing through a lane of oaks, through the old sandstone cliff country—ancient Aeolian ridges of cross-bedded dunes from a time when the highest known form of life was invertebrates—I happened but to glance up and see that a pack of young coyotes was watching me, each one drenched, as if they'd been out hunting all morning. Each one was camouflaged almost perfectly against the reddish-gray cliffs.

It wasn't even the coyotes themselves I saw, at first, but instead a faintly different line in the crossbedding—the cant of an ear running at a forty-five degree angle against the strike of the bedding plane, and then a wet black button of a nose, and then another nose, and another; more ears, and then a pair of sentient eyes set back in the stone: eyes everywhere, I saw suddenly, until I counted five young coyotes watching me, all frozen in various positions of watchfulness.

I stopped and stood there in the falling rain, amazed at their naivete—did they not know, even if only by the instinct of their much-persecuted kind, that there were others of my kind, vertical human beings, looking not all that different from me, who would just as lief begin firing into their midst, as look at them? People who might believe that one more dead coyote might equal one more living deer, or that one more dead coyote might somehow equal a better day?

After what seemed like a long time, but was probably only seconds, they turned and broke and ran, scattering into the brush. And I kept on walking home, through the brush and through the steady rain, trying to hunt, but beginning to daydream—as if by seeing all those coyotes, something inside me had been filled, and I no longer wanted a deer, or anything, but was content with the world and my place in it, precisely the way things were. Boots squishing, hair drenched, fingers wet and cold. It was all just right, just perfect; one more day.

RUSSELL'S ONLY A FEW years younger than I am, but he hasn't hit the midlife wall yet: like any of us, he's happy just to be out on the landscape, but unlike the old graybeards we're so quickly becoming, he really, really wants a deer. Already, he's passed up an easy shot at a decent six-point buck on the first day, waiting for something larger, and already, in retrospect, he's been ruing his choice. If we've heard him say it once, we've heard him say it a hundred times, with a shake of his head, on this hunt, "Dang, I shouldn't have passed that buck up." And, of course, his older brothers, Rick and Randy, are merciless, responding not with any tender words of support or understanding and affirmation, but instead bobbing their heads gleefully and agreeing with his misery wholeheartedly, chorusing "Thass right! Thass right!" And when Russell glowers at them, totally abandoned, totally deer-less, they'll leap up from their seats on the couch and walk back outside to go examine their deer, which are hanging from the meat pole, and they'll make a big point of trying to out-brag each other on the other's deer—Rick complimenting Randy on the long brow tines over his deer, for instance, and the body size, while Randy pretends not to hear any of it and instead declaims loudly, for all to hear, about the beautiful mahogany color and impressive width of the antlers on Rick's deer. Brothers!

EACH DAY SINCE that first day, Russell has gone out with an increasing sense of mission and commitment, and, to his credit, he hasn't been shy about camouflaging it. *I really want a deer*, he says each morning; and throughout the pasture, we listen for a single shot from his .270, but hear nothing—and each evening, back in camp, sitting around the woodstove inside, sipping a vodka-and-tonic while the rain drums ever harder on the roof, he seems glummer and glummer, though to his credit again, always he wrestles with his frustration, remembers his priority, and shrugs and says, "Well, anyway, it's great to be here with everyone together again, that's all that really matters"—a statement with which the two Asshole Brothers will enthusiastically agree, just before jumping up and running back outside to comment loudly and favorably once more on each other's deer.

LATE ON THE THIRD DAY—the next-to-last day—Russell finally gets a deer, and that night he is utterly radiant with a beatific mix of joy and relief. It's a nice big fat deer, a fine, gnarly eight-point, and after supper, while sitting around the woodstove later in the evening, he tells us again how the hunt went. He's been reliving it all afternoon, thrilled by his good fortune, and even though I know exactly what he's feeling—I felt that way as recently as a year or two ago—there's still a bit of an odd feeling for me, like being on a boat, I think, that is pulling away from shore: like looking back at others who are not on the boat, but who have remained behind, still standing on the dock from which you departed, and with a distance accruing even as you look back.

I can see and know his pleasure, joy, excitement, happiness, pride, relief, but I can no longer quite grasp it. I do not feel any older than I did last year physically, but the boat is pulling away and that distance is widening, even if painlessly.

"I was already heading in to lunch," Russell said. "I had my gun slung over my shoulder and was packing it in, when this nice buck with really dark antlers ran right in front of me and then stopped about fifty yards out and turned back and looked at me. I knelt down and put the scope on him, but he was turned around and looking right at me, so that all I could see was his neck, and I didn't have a brace. My gun was wavering a little bit. Maybe I should have shot, but I kept waiting for him to turn broadside.

"Then I heard Uncle Charlie coming up the road in the jeep. The deer bolted and went over the hill. I was kicking myself, thinking maybe I should have taken the shot, that I'd blown the only other chance I'd get the whole hunt.

"I could hear the jeep coming. I figured that deer was long gone, but I decided to hurry on up over the hill before the jeep got to me, to see if the buck might have stopped on the other side of the hill.

"I didn't think I had a chance in a million, but when I got over the hill, there he was, standing in the rain, back in the mesquite, about seventy-five yards away. I didn't waste any time, but braced against the crotch of a tree—the jeep was really close now—and squeezed. He dropped like a rock," Russell said, with that relief and happiness and wonder—that completeness—filling his voice again: the utter improbability of having wanted something badly, and having gone out after it, against the odds, and being successful. Mostly luck; almost all luck. Any hunter knows that. And yet, that's the best part: as if in the end it was the sharpness of your desire—your need—that delivered the animal to you. That allowed the animal to be delivered to you.

It's an awful lot like prayer. It's not a prayer exactly, or precisely, I don't think, but then again, maybe it is. You don't really come right out and ask for it—well, almost never—but you come right to the edge of that ask. And then you hold that desire, and hold it, as if carrying a great iron weight; and then it is as if a door or gate opens, and what you desired is delivered to you, often in seemingly miraculous fashion, as if to underscore your undeservingness, and the strange wild mercy of the gift.

I remember it. And I remember how it feels back in camp, or back home, after such a day: that first night back from the land of miracles.

THAT SAME DAY, Randy has secured something maybe even finer, in my mind, and after Russell finishes his story, Randy, in the quiet way that he has, shows us the handful of arrowheads he's found, the points exposed from beneath the thin soil due to the erosion from the sustained and heavy rains, the past re-made and resurrected. Any one of the arrowheads is enough to make us exclaim, enough to make me jump up and shout my admiration with an enthusiasm that might be summoned by me now for only the most amazing buck, and Randy smiles and shrugs.

I REMEMBER A DEER I wanted badly, a long time ago; could it have been fifteen years, maybe more? It was the second or third morning, we did not yet have any deer in camp, and there had been a hard frost that night. The woods were glittering, autumn-dead grass spangled with diamonds, and as I sat crouched within a mot of old oaks, I saw a nice buck come walking through the oaks, his nose wet and bright black in the cold, his eyes glistening dark in the morning sun, his breath leaving him in twin plumes. He stopped, sensing something, and just stood there, breathing. His coat was acorn fat, and I could not remember having ever seen a more beautiful deer. He wasn't a trophy, just a big handsome deer on the most beautiful morning of the year.

I eased the rifle up and placed him in the scope. It was the same scope through which my grandfather had squinted at countless deer. I squeezed the trigger, breaking the frozen morning, and the deer jumped, hunchbacked, as they will sometimes do when hit. He didn't fall, however, nor did he run. Instead, he just stood there, between me and the rising ball of the sun, stock-still, and I could see a third plume rising from him, not the twin-pulse of his nostrils' breath, but a steady steaming, like smoke from a chimney. I had creased the top of his back, a flesh wound. With the sun in his eyes and the report of the rifle so loud, he was not sure what had happened.

It was just the faintest paper-cut of a wound.

I raised the rifle, disbelieving at my good fortune to have a second chance, braced more firmly, took a breath, exhaled as I squeezed the trigger, and he collapsed. I have never cared for the phrase "never knew what hit him"—a graceless way of acknowledging every hunter's goal—but while other, more eloquent phrases might be crafted, the goal does remain the same, and when I walked up to examine the deer, he was already over on the other side, while I was still here, and gifted with bounty.

THERE'S A SLIGHT BREAK in the rain, finally, the next-to-last night, and we're able to have a campfire, another long-standing tradition—sitting out on the porch, or around the campfire ring, watching the stars and telling the old stories and trying out new ones.

When my cousins and I were all children, Randy, who was hell-on-wheels with his Havahart live trap, was forever capturing wild things and attempting to domesticate them. I seem to recall him almost always in one state of bandaging or another, swathed like a mummy sometimes, from where he had been bitten: by rabbits, snakes both poisonous and non, raccoons, owls, skunks—he caught it all, and it all bit him.

This evening, we're reminiscing about some of the raccoons of our childhood: Randy's raccoons. Weecha. Ajax. Miss Phyllis.

"That Ajax was the mean one," Russell says, his voice dreamy. "My God, I hadn't thought about that sonofabitch in over thirty years. That was the one that would chase me down when I was little and start chewing on me, with me too little to fight back, and you just standing there laughing, like some Dark Lord or something, right? What was I, five, six, maybe seven years old?"

Randy smiles. "He was a mean one," he says.

"Who named him?" I ask. "Who was he named for?" Randy and Russell look at each other with puzzlement. They once knew, but now can't remember; and the surprise on their faces, that they could possibly have forgotten such a vital fact, is interesting to me, bittersweet.

EVEN AS IT'S A BIT OF A BUMMER to see how quickly my cousins and I are marching into the years, one of the real pleasures of this year's hunt is to see how much responsibility the youngest among us, B. J., is assuming. His birthday is the first of November—the first week of deer season—and he's fifteen years younger than I am. We used to joke about how one day he'd be the one running the camp, taking care of a bunch of old folks—cooking, cleaning, and toting our deer, patching leaks in the cabin, repairing broken water pumps—but darned if he's not already there, and enjoying it. It's strange and nice to be content to just lean back in the lawn chair and sip a drink at the end of a long and physical day and listen to the rustling sounds of B. J. down in the brush, foraging for firewood and then hauling it up the hill.

He gathers great funeral-pyre quantities of it, and then—like Old Grand-daddy, from whose block he is chipped—a sonic-boom whoosh turns the night briefly to day.

And every morning, he's the first one up, padding cold-footed across the floor to get the coffee going—the hissing, percolating sounds of it awaken-ing us with the reminder that everything's all right, B. J. is here—and each morning, even in this incredible spell of rain, he somehow has a cheery fire blazing in our little woodstove, having pirated away tiny damp twigs and kindling from the day before, which he dried all evening in front of our one-watt electrical heater (whose range is confined exclusively to the bathroom), in front of which are also stacked, each evening, our charred and smoldering socks and steaming boots, like burnt offerings at an altar, the boots never quite drying out in time for the next day's use, but warming and contracting slightly, the leather tongues twisting like the carcasses of roadstruck crea-tures along a desert highway, so that we must grunt and struggle each next-morning, laboring to pull them on.

It's so awesome to be proud of one's younger family members. It's such powerful antidote against the sometimes haunting tally or inventory of the fading or rounding of one's own enthusiasms. Sometimes I feel like an old person in a rest home, staring slack-jawed at and spellbound by the vitality of youth, remembering, *I was there—just last year, I was there, I can see how much joy the world brings you, and I used to be there every minute of every day . . .*

It is not that the world no longer brings joy, or wonder—it still does, and with even more of the latter than ever.

I'm not quite sure what it is I'm trying to say. Something about the force of that joy, I think, or maybe the randomness of it: being made joyful and alive by getting up early on a cold morning and getting a crackling fire going before anyone else is up.

I remember that kind of wild and random force of joy, and what is sweet-est and most hopeful of all, I think, is the realization that I can still get there—that it is still within reach, on any given day, as long as I remember not to take the world, or anything else, for granted.

BERT, WHO LIVES ON the property adjacent to ours, and who helps look after ours too, during the many long months of absence, comes by at lunch on the fourth and last full day of hunting. It's a beautiful crisp blue day, with the rain finally breaking, and we saw some animals, even a few small bucks, though nothing anyone wanted to shoot.

Bert always comes on the last day during lunch, to sip a Coke and check out the deer we've been fortunate enough to find, and, in essence, to say hello and good-bye at the same time. He's friendly, but respects our privacy. He understands what the hunt is about for us these days. And although he's only in his late fifties, it seems he's been here forever. Certainly he's been here long enough to have known us back when we really used to like to kill deer, and he has watched that transformation come over us, one by one, wherein the importance of the deer has receded (as it has for him) ever further. He has a sharp eye for such things, and he knows, can tell just in a glance, who among us the shadow has not yet crossed over: in this year's case, the two youngest, Russell and B. J.

Before coming inside, he walks over to the deer-skinning pole and looks at our paltry take: remembering, doubtless, the old days, when eight hunters would surely have hanging at least eight nice bucks, and maybe more. (The limit is two bucks per hunter.)

Three this year; all nice deer, it's true, but three deer for seven hunters?

Bert's got the worst kind of a sense of humor—or rather, that best and most difficult kind, where he's so damned serious and earnest almost all of the time that when he truly does happen onto a piece of humor, he guards it deliciously, frugal as a Scot, and only gives it out to you in tiny pieces, so that often it might be ten or fifteen minutes after he's finished talking before you even begin to understand that humor's been delivered. And this is how it is this last day at lunch, as he stands there admiring the deer. He spends a lot of time out on the pasture and it's always of interest to us to see if he recognizes the deer we've been fortunate enough to take.

Usually, with most of the deer, he recognizes them—nods at each of them, as if they were near-strangers of only passing acquaintance—though sometimes there will be a deer he's never seen before, and he'll stand before that one a little longer, studying it, and wondering, always, if it was just some shy and totally nocturnal deer, one that had kept successfully out of sight for years, not even showing itself in the headlights when Bert would come driving back in from town at night, or if the unknown mystery deer was some unfortunate wayfarer, merely passing through, who simply found himself in the wrong place at the wrong time.

This year, Bert is standing before Russell's buck in that manner, or so it seems to us, even though Russell's buck is not the largest of the three. It's a pretty deer, all right, but it seems to me that Bert's spending a dispropor-tionate, perhaps even inordinate amount of time before that deer—though finally, after staring at it just a little longer, he grunts, and then comes on in through the screen door. He doesn't know who shot which deer: that part comes later, after he's caught us up on all the year's doings, and we likewise, and when there are fewer things to talk about. That's when he might gesture toward Rick's nice big fat deer and say, "Who got that eight-point? I've been seeing him running does on the east side for the last week," or something like that.

And that's how it goes this year—antlered-deer chitchat—and then, after the briefest of Bert-pauses—you would have to have known him for a life-time to know that some sort of bedevilment is up, and of the best sort—the true, the found, the unmanipulated.

"You know that seven-point hanging out there?" Bert begins, tentative-ly—and like the wariest, wildest of creatures, Russell tenses, understanding somehow intuitively that he does not want to hear what it is that Bert has to say, and that furthermore, he, Russell, does not want the rest of us to hear whatever it is that Bert, clarion-caller of the truth, has to say.

As Bert begins with his own intuitions and observations to under-stand that it's Russell's deer (tipped off, perhaps, by the paleness of Rus-sell's face), he proceeds cautiously. And is it my imagination, or does a deeper flicker of amusement cross Bert's almost sorrowful or at least straightforward-reporting expression? A jumble of emotions, and all so carefully moderated. In the end, he decides to put Russell out of his misery quickly. "I used to feed that little deer," he says. Bert's not a harsh man, but he's a countryman, a good hand: he's birthed and buried as many animals as anyone and lives daily in the life-and-death cycle of nature. "Two years ago, he was sort of my pet," Bert says. And again, there's the strange mix of sorrow and yet devilment: knowing, of course, that it is the nature of male deer to be shot—if not this November, then the next, or surely the next. "Last year he went over to some other folks' property, where there weren't any hunters," he said. *Away from the likes of you,* he might as well have said. Not angry: just matter-of-fact. Life on the farm.

What's worst of all, perhaps, is that Bert's not trying to drive the knife in further. He's just spilling the truth: compelled to testify, it seems, upon this most sorrowful of reunions.

"I used to feed him grain from a bucket," Bert says. "I don't know why he was so tame. He'd hear my truck and come running from halfway across the pasture to meet me." Bert shakes his head dolefully and then, worst of all, seems to truly reach deep, as if trying to buck up and be a rancher about all this. "I guess those days are gone now," he says, trying to make a little wry rancher joke. He smiles ruefully, as if to tell us *Don't feel bad, fellas, some other hunter would have gotten him anyway*—and with that, he nods, shakes our hands, and we trade our good-byes, telling him that we'll see him next season.

On the way out to his truck, he glances only briefly once more at the nice buck.

LATER THAT AFTERNOON, we can't help ourselves. Cousin Rick is the first to approach the subject, which all day long has been lingering just beneath the surface, like the shadow of a fish, barely seen.

"When Charlie and Jimmy came driving up the hill," he speculates—addressing Russell—"and your deer went running over the hill—he must have stopped and let you catch up because he thought the truck, the jeep, was Daddy Bert, after all those years, coming back with another bucket of grain.

Their jeep sounds just like his old truck," Rick says, and Russell just shakes his head, having known the shit was coming, and seeming almost relieved, perhaps, that it is finally beginning. Still, he looks a little glum, and I feel compelled to speak the obvious.

"Aww, Russell, he was a wild buck. That was a long time ago . . ."

"Don't patronize him," Randy snaps, mock wild-eyed, and we all laugh, even Russell, though still, it is a head-shaking, disbelieving laugh, an Aw-shit-I-can't-believe-what-I-stepped-in laugh—and yet, as any of us would be the first to admit, he was a very fine deer, a fine handsome specimen of a buck, and there is always luck involved, luck and the desires of the world always trump skill, and we find ourselves in possession of still another story to trade back and forth with each other, sanding and polishing and refining, across the coming decades, and I think we're each more than a little grateful that it's Russell's, and not our own.

I know already that in future years we will be passing this story back and forth, passing it around like another arrowhead, with the sight but also the touch of each flaked edge pleasing, each of us touching and handling and even slightly altering, in each re-telling, the worked ridges of the artifact itself, until it is shaped just right, and some more elegant version of the truth—if not entirely the original facts—might emerge.

WE FINISH OUR LUNCH with the awe of having been given—handed—a story—all of us except Russell, that is—and I don't know what it is, but something about the incredible blue sky, and the quality of crisp dry November light, and the familiar sounds and scents of midday camp, and the unexpected arrival of story, conspire to reconnect me to older memories, and to this place, and to my own place among my family. And while each year's November hunt is no longer about making game, about securing meat, I finally feel, for the first time of the entire trip, like a deer hunter, instead of a vacationer—and I am aware of keenly desiring to hunt one.

The fact that it is so late in the hunt—the last day—seems only to sweeten the desire. Better for it to return late than not at all; and who knows, I tell myself, this might be the last time. Maybe there comes a point where the desire never comes back, but passes on to other, younger hunters. Who knows what contract, what negotiation, exists in the world between the spirits of the hunters and the hunted?

I'm so pleased with the return of desire that I announce it to my cousins, father, uncle, brothers. "I'd love to find an animal," I say, being cautious, in my backwoods way, not to say the animal's name, *deer*—much less the specificity of "a nice buck"—in order to keep from presuming arrogance. Understanding, eventually, how much luck is involved with every animal. A seeming paradox: the more "successful" a hunter becomes, the more he or she realizes it is all built upon a scaffolding of luck, or chance, or some other third thing, that invisible and inaudible contract of spirit wherein, if your desire is sustained and intense and pure enough, the animal will sometimes appear for a moment as if summoned, or even as if offering itself—or at least the chance, the opportunity—to the subject of that desire: the desire.

You might have heard such things before, and dismissed them at first as New Age mumbo jumbo, but ultimately, if you take enough animals, you come to a point where you can't deny it, and where instead you come to know it. The improbability of Russell catching back up with that deer after it ran off the first time; the improbability of a young hunter being presented with a shot at a magnificent animal, and making it, even as the other older, more veteran hunters receive no such presentation; the improbability of a hunter who, deeply desiring an animal and having hunted hard all season long, is occasionally presented with an opportunity at dusk on the last day of the season . . .

There's something up, out there in the woods, a thing that our scientists and atom-chasers and neutron-smashers will likely never be able to prove or discover—a braided spirit, is what it seems like to me—and sometimes a hunter finds him- or herself inside it, and other times, outside it. It exists, though what to make of such knowledge, I am not quite sure, other than to try to remember, always, to say please and thank you.

I SET OFF UP THE HILL WITH my grandfather's old rifle, after everyone— cousins, brothers, father, uncle—had wished me good luck. The whole hunt,

I had not really been wanting an animal (which may be why I had not seen one), but now, on this last afternoon, the desire had returned. For seventy-five-plus years, our family's been hunting this land—it was my twenty-fifth year to hunt it—and these days, often, I prefer to just hike around instead of hunt.

So it was a joy to feel so sharply that yearning, and that pressure: to be forced, by the last-chance nature of my schedule, to stalk so quietly, so carefully—to be so *alive*—through the dense dark shade of the cedar, which was where the deer would be bedded down, this hot dry sunny windy afternoon. Creeping through the thickest tangles, moving slowly and almost silently.

And in my stalk, I began to see the deer that I had not been seeing earlier. Or rather, I was seeing them before they saw me this time, and beneath the low tangled dark canopy of the cedar, with the boughs above whipping and waving in the wind, I was seeing them at extremely close range: a liquid brown eye widening at fifteen yards, also alive; the incandescent illumination of whiskers, light-filled from a thin beam of sun that made it somehow down into the canopy; the lower jaw of a doe, grinding something, chewing . . .

They were all does. I was searching for the drama of antlers. The does were all beautiful, and I knew the meat would be delicious, but I was looking for those bone-hardened antlers of mahogany, the crown or candelabra.

And in part, it wasn't even as if I was looking for a deer, but instead, as if I was just walking carefully, stalking, more intent upon preserving that desire, rather than desiring the deer, if that makes any sense.

TIME SEEMED TO DOUBLE in density, slowing and then vanishing. In my mind, there was only the next step, and each step was more vital than any of the previous, for it would do no good to be silent with all the other steps only to then crack a twig or dislodge a clattering pebble, ruining with that one act all of the earlier investment of silence. I forgot to look at my watch, and even forgot that this was the last afternoon of the last day of the hunt. Instead, I was aware only of timelessness. The landscape before me was as familiar as it had ever been, across the decades, but it seemed also as if I'd entered a new territory—the same land, but in a different era, and whether that era might be the past or the future, I couldn't say.

This day, I was just looking for antlers: for a hidden animal that won't see me.

I'd been walking even slower, being so cautious not to ruin the afternoon's stalk. My wanting continued to escalate, until I found myself doing something I rarely do, and never gratuitously: asking the hills for an animal. I hesitated to call it a prayer, but truth be told, that's pretty close to what it's like. It's kind of a semi-urgent, yet utterly respectful asking—a *Come on, please, I really want this animal*. Not a negotiation—not, *If I get this animal, I'll share it with other folks who aren't fortunate enough to have procured meat*; no *If I get this animal, I'll promise to work harder on behalf of the woods.*

Instead, rather than prayer or plea bargain, it's more like a submission and a demand both: a submission to the understanding that the animal will not be delivered to the hunter without some intervention, and a demand, an insistence, that the world (and perhaps the animal itself) hear and understand more clearly the fuller weight of the hunter's desire.

And yet, how can the animal hear such a demand, for has not the hunter—up until this point—been extraordinarily cautious to avoid alerting the animal to the hunter's desire, and the hunter's presence? How can a thing be two things at once, *aware* and *unaware*? Or is it in that transition of prayer—if we agree to call it such—that the animal lifts its head and turns and stares back as if into infinity, and decides, or is compelled by other forces, to agree to such a contract?

A part of you wants to reject completely such an idea. And yet, if you have gone after such animals—into the brush, into the forest—you know that this is often how it is, and that it happens too often, it cannot possibly be coincidence. Something else is happening, even if you do not quite know what.

And maybe it's more like a yearning than a true prayer—an imploring, a heartfelt request—sometimes even a beseeching. Whatever it is, you can't just go around doing it all the time. The moment has to be right, so much so that perhaps the asking is not even your idea, but rather, is initiated from outside forces.

Key to part of it also, I believe, is that you have to have put in the miles, and be tired, even weary, and near the end of your limits, before you even consider making such an outlandish ask—the life of another animal. You have to be absolutely certain you want it; you have to have been tested. And I don't know what the other part of it is.

THAT MORNING, I HAD awakened around three, had arisen and fixed coffee, and sat at the table in the kitchen and worked by flashlight on my novel. In it, I had come to a scene, a passage, in which some sojourners are traveling over a high mountain pass in the Himalayas. They're starving, on their way down into Burma to try to capture an elephant, and one of the travelers sets out to look for a blue sheep, which is the only game to be found that high in the mountains. And in the novel, the hunter made his little prayer, and a blue sheep was delivered to him, encountered at dusk.

If this seems like an indulgent digression, forgive me. It was a part of my 3:00 a.m. dream-life and certainly was no longer on my mind. And yet surely it must also have still been within me, for as I was creeping down a dark shady narrow canyon, the pitch and plunge of the creek so steep that it formed a laddered series of waterfalls, I paused behind a tree for some unknown reason, and a few seconds later an animal came sneaking up the creek, its muscles and sandstone-colored coat and horns glinting in the light.

The animal was deer-sized, as it passed through a beam of gold sunlight that filtered down through the cool shady canopy, and yet it was not a deer; and after my first initial surge of joy and excitement—*Thank you*, I was already whispering, thrilled by the wildness of the gift—the animal was very close, and yet was still unaware of me—I felt a moment of slight letdown, and felt off-balance. Is it a yearling bull-calf, I wondered, a feral escapee from some other ranch?

Then the rest of the herd shifted into focus, giant aoudads, or Barbary sheep, with full-curled horns, and each looking as large as an elk—utter, secret wildness—and I decided that the hunt was back on again.

I had seen aoudads back in the cliffs before. The first ones escaped from Hill Country game farms more than two decades ago, and found the rocky, arid region similar enough to their native African home that they survived and, said some, even prospered, sometimes displacing white-tailed deer.

On two occasions when I'd seen them, I'd had no interest in shooting one, even though I knew that a purer hunter might not have given such a thought a second's pause. They were not native to the landscape and in that regard could be said to be like weeds or pests—and yet, they seemed to me also to be like strangers, even guests, rather than prey, and because they had not even been remotely in my search-image—only deer and turkey—it would have been as unthinkable for me to take one, then, as to shoot a dog or a cat, a parakeet or flamingo, a crane or coyote, simply because I saw them.

Both times, I watched them clatter away, deft-hoofed, disappearing into slots between boulders—vanishing, as if in a dream. Was I still in Texas, or now the Moorish Coast?

WHAT MAKES A NATIVE? And how much of such a definition rests in the contract of fit negotiated between species and landscape, and how much in the eye of beholder? And how much in the eye of time?

I had not gone out hunting for wild sheep—they had not even been in my consciousness—but here, moments after asking for an animal, came an entire herd, so stealthy and wild that my desire did not wane, but was sharpened, and as the entire herd moved one by one through that column of sun and then back into the shadow, with the music of the laddered waterfall filling that tight little canyon, I did my choosing and decided to pass on the larger animals, which I recognized as certain trophies, and to instead take the younger animal, which would surely taste good. I had not asked for a three hundred-pound animal and was not going to take one.

The smaller animal—a two-year-old?—had long horns that were only beginning to curl. He was very close—I could see the sunlight wet-like in his brown eyes, could see his strange beard—and when I shot, he fell instantly, landing in the shallow little creek.

The rest of the herd froze for a second, not knowing where the shot had come from. Then they saw or scented me and whirled and crashed off through the brush, cracking limbs and branches like a herd of frightened elk, and again I said *thank you*, not just for the gift of wild meat, but for such a wonderful hunt—and then I walked down the creek to where the sheep lay, some blood trickling into the clear stone creek like a sacrifice, and I said *thank you* again, and pulled him out of the water and up the slope into the dense forest, where I examined him then like a scientist, astounded by such a specimen—such uniqueness, after all my life having hunted only deer and turkey on this land. And once again I felt as if I was in the midst of time-lessness, and yet also as if I had ridden on the back of some great passage of time—centuries, perhaps—for the animals at the deer pasture to have changed so.

And as with some of the stories told often by my father and grandfather and uncle, so familiar that sometimes it seemed, in the listening, as if I had lived them myself, I could not be sure if what I felt was that I had traveled forward, or backward. But I felt somehow that I had traveled.

The sun was setting red against a shoal of clouds. The music of the water-fall was still beautiful. I had been given an animal *and* a story. I cleaned the animal with care, washed my hands in the cold water of the creek, then rose and hiked back to camp in the red dusk, thinking things over.

THE ANIMAL HAD BEEN KILLED a long way from a road—in the farthest, deepest canyon possible—so that hauling him out at night was going to be an adventure for a bunch of middle-aged guys, and one I looked forward to. The stars were out, and the night was cold enough that he would have been fine where he was, but I kept thinking about the five coyotes I'd seen in the area, the day before. And it was a sweet feeling, walking back to camp with my hands washed, my knife clean in its sheath, and with meat for the com-ing year, and having received the animal in such strange, wild fashion. One of the best hunts ever.

It felt good to be hiking out, climbing the steep rocky hills, and feeling the same strength in my legs that had always been there, and feeling my lungs reach deep to fill with air. Forty-five's not old. There are good days and bad days—a good day reminding you of how you felt when you were, say, twenty-five, and a bad day seeming like a harbinger, perhaps, of what the body might be like at fifty-five, or even sixty-five, compromised, and reduced—but today was a good day, and my relationship with the steep hills seemed as secure as it always had been, for one more evening at least. And I was old enough now to know to treasure that sensation, and at the top of the last hill I paused for a moment not to catch my breath, but to simply admire the evening's first stars.

BACK IN CAMP, they could tell something was up. Supper was already cooking, and when someone comes in late like that, it's usually because they were out later than expected, cleaning an animal. They inspected my hands and knife for blood, but found none. They had not heard the shot from down in the slot canyon, but somehow, they knew: and when they asked if I'd gotten anything, I said that yes I had, that it was just a spike—that his antlers "had no tines"—but that he was a big one and that I was very happy with him, very fortunate and lucky to have encountered him.

I don't know how they could tell something was up, but they could. After all the years of jokes and stories, the successes and failures, we can read each other like the blood kin we are—as if the shared blood still communicates, despite being housed in separate vessels. It was my cousins' opinion that I had shot a huge buck and was only pretending it was a spike, so that they would be surprised when they saw it. They refused to believe I'd shoot a spike, even as I insisted that this was a fine animal, a really big one.

Cousin Rick—well-versed in the ways of pranks and larceny himself—was working hard to get to the heart of the matter. He knew I wouldn't lie to them, but they all knew somehow that I was holding a secret, a surprise.

"Okay, Richard," he said, attempting to wade to the bottom of it. "Look at my hand." He held it up vertically like the needle on some calibrated scale. "This is the bullshit meter. Now: *Did you shoot a spike?*"

Yes. Said firmly. The hand wavered but did not tilt.

"You bushwhacked way to the back side and that's where the animal is still lying?"

Yes. No wobble.

"The animal is not a trophy buck."

No. Again, no waver.

"Is there any bullshit associated with this story?"

Pause. *Yes.*

Rick laughed and shook his head. "You see?" he told his brothers. "The bullshit meter works."

They frowned, then protested. "You didn't get anything out of him that he hadn't already told us."

Rick shrugged. "But now you know it's the truth."

"But your last question—he himself admitted it was bullshit . . ."

Rick just shrugged, laughed again. "But *true* bullshit," he explained.

"The worst kind," I said.

WE SAT DOWN TO OUR BIG blow-out dinner, the kind that will likely be outlawed by heart surgeons in twenty years—big grilled steaks, big baked potatoes with real butter, real sour cream, real bacon, real cheese. Where did the hunt go, how can another one be over so fast?

After dinner, Rick and my father were the only ones sporting enough to sally out in search of the animal. I had drawn on a napkin a map of the general place where the animal lay, though my understanding of where the looping, grassed-over dirt roads wandered in relation to that canyon was admittedly inaccurate, and there seemed to be no one place any closer to the animal than another.

The plan we settled upon in the end was for my father to stay with the jeep, with the headlights burning, and Rick and I would bushwhack up the creek, find the animal, and then triangulate out in the shortest, most direct route toward those headlights, dragging and carrying the animal through the brush.

We had not gone more than two minutes into the brush before the glow of the jeep headlights disappeared completely.

Still, we pushed on, climbing small cliffs and descending little canyons— half a dozen or more little creeks and canyons, over on the back side— thrashing and struggling through eye-level cedar boughs, spitting out bark and berries, dropping our flashlights and stumbling and tripping, veering north then south, east then west, as I tried to recognize in the darkness individual trees and rocks.

After about half an hour, I seemed to recognize a change in the melody of the creek, a familiar tune now, and shining my light on the ground, I saw a spot of blood where the animal had fallen and a few loose hairs from where I had dragged him up on the hill away from the creek.

Rick was sweating and stumbling too, about to give up the faith, but when I called him over to look at the animal and he saw what it was, he was properly excited, and understood too, I think, that it was as if we were witnessing some strange cleaving, a Part One and Part Two in our family's relationship to this place, and the hunt. We'd killed hundreds of deer—maybe a thousand—across all the decades, but never anything like this, and he, too, knelt and gave, with the curiosity of his examination, the animal his own respect.

AN HOUR LATER, we had the animal out to a road, though it was not the road we had left from, and we could see on the next mountain over the headlights of my father's jeep. Having understandably given up on the possibility that we would be coming out at the same spot where we had entered the woods, he had begun driving up and down the sand roads looking for us, certain that we were lost, and we shone our flashlights over toward the little mountain he was on, unsure whether he would even see their firefly-blinkings; though after a while, he turned the jeep around and answered our lights with blinks of his own and circled around to find the grassy road that would take him to where we sat with our strange quarry, visiting, reliving the hunt, and marveling at how even a world that seems more familiar to you than anything is always capable of delivering a surprise.

Not frequently, perhaps, but always, such possibility exists. Sometimes for the asking, and other times, whether you ask or not.

BACK IN CAMP, there was, to my way of thinking, appropriate marveling at the appearance of such a strange creature—an ambassador from the future—and, in the story-telling that accompanied his arrival, a foundation that would one day—next year, already—become the past, our past. We understood that fifty or sixty years from now our own sons and daughters and nieces and nephews—if they still cared about such things, and about this place, with even remotely the same intensity as we do—might be curious as to when and how, roughly, the first animal was taken. It seemed significant to us, a reflector of the natural history of the place—an artifact, already, and a story, already, which we were sure we would pass back and forth, shaping and re-shaping.

A hundred years ago, even the juniper upon which the animal browsed had not been here, save for a few smatterings. Everything changes, even the shape of the hills themselves, beneath the millennia of wind and fire and running water. The aoudad was not a huge animal, hanging there next to the deer in camp, with the strange dark stripe down its back, its long crenulated horns, its odd tail and its strange circus-beard. But it felt huge, in a way we could not quite place.

I think each of us suspected that one day, looking back, we would be able to come closer to explaining that feeling. But that night, and the next morning, as we cleaned our animals and packed up to leave, all we knew to do was to make it and the rest of the hunt into another story, or stories, and to pass them back and forth, shaping them already, even as we knew also it was more the tellers than the stories themselves who were being shaped.

MARY KATHERINE'S
FIRST DEER

YOU CAN'T PUSH HER, any more than you can push her mother—and it occurs to me only now that in this regard I too may share some responsibility for my oldest daughter's character. I'm trying to avoid using the *s* word, "stubborn," but really can't see much way around it. The word I'm trying to think of would have more positive and pleasant connotations than "headstrong," "willful," or "stubborn." I don't know what that word would be, but I know that it can often describe Mary Katherine.

She took her hunter's certification test when she was eleven, mostly because her friends were taking it, I think—in rural northwestern Montana, rarely is a family without at least one hunter—but in the year following that, she chose not to go hunting, though I had imagined that it would be quite fine to take her into the woods early in the mornings in the autumn, and particularly after a new snow was down, and particularly up into the high country, to look for, and perhaps follow, a deer or an elk. Not so much to find one, but to follow one, and draw nearer to it: to know that passion.

I think, however, it might have been a little off-putting: the way I had come in from the hunt so many times frozen or ragged, drenched and soggy, and the way, at each season's end, my feet were blistered and tattered. I would tell her it didn't have to be that way, but she didn't seem eager to go try it, and whether that was the reason, or the killing was the reason, or any of a braid of a hundred others, I couldn't quite tell, and didn't probe too much, and sure know better than to push. Twelve *is* awfully young, even in Montana.

That autumn passed, and a couple of her friends were fortunate enough to find, and shoot, a deer. I exclaimed my pleasure to them, offered my congratulations, and we traveled on into her thirteenth year.

We still went over to the east side of the state, bird hunting as we always had, a couple of times each year—Mary Katherine and Lowry, neither of them carrying guns, but walking behind me and the dogs, wading the prairie beneath that huge sky, following the dogs as if harnessed to them, and them helping me flush the birds when the dogs went on point—but still there was no desire by Mary Katherine to go after deer or elk, with or even without rifle in hand.

Thirteen years old is not always the greatest age for togetherness between any child and parent, and my mantra, as I watched her beginning to grow up quickly, became *Meet her where she is*. Not to spoil her, and not to overcrowd her, and not to push her, but still, to remain vigilant and be present, and to watch for the opportunity to simply remain somewhat in her life and to pretty much forget, for the time being, about having her in *my* life—within the borders and boundaries of my own passions—as had been the sweet and wonderful case once-upon-a-time, and for a long while.

Those days were gone, and the trick, the task—the opportunity—was to find sweetness in these new days: for surely it was there, too, simply in different form and fashion. After a long period of not growing, I would be asked—or presented the opportunity—to grow, too. Not as fast as she was—no one, save her peers, could keep up with that. But to grow again, after a long time of not: as if I had been out wandering the mountains and had crossed over into another valley, one unfamiliar to me.

If I am making it sound like the position of fatherhood in such a time is somewhat akin to that of an old hound sitting around on the porch waiting to be let back in, certainly, there are days when that's pretty much how it is. Watching, and waiting.

THE SEASON OF HER thirteenth year passed—I continued to let her know that anytime she changed her mind, I'd be happy to take her out to look for an animal, for any period of time—but she had not even bought a license, and seemed by now to have pretty much made her peace with the decision that she didn't want to hunt. She wasn't opposed to it, by any means; she just didn't have that spark in her. And while I would have liked for her to have that spark, I accepted her choice as part of the wonderful young woman she would become, was becoming.

Late in October, a friend of hers went out with her older sister's boyfriend and was fortunate enough to take a cow elk.

The rut began in mid-November, and a couple of boys at her school were fortunate enough to find some bucks.

The snow was down by this time.

"I think I can find you an animal," I said. "We could just go out for an hour or so." Pushing, again. Hoping, again, I guess.

She shook her head. She didn't yell at me, didn't shout "Leave me alone!" But it was still a no.

Thanksgiving came—the peak of drama, for the hunting season—deep cold, and wild deer, elk, turkey on the table, celebrated, and time spent away from school, deep in the heart of home, and deep in the heart of the valley— and I continued to wander out each day, just looking around to see what I might see. I had been very fortunate to find a young bull after a long hard season of hunting and had just finished packing him all out, so that we were not short on meat. I was hunting with leisure, as such, rather than deepest need.

The season was winding down. That weekend—that Saturday—I decided to float the offer out there one last time, ever so casually. There was a light snow predicted, and for whatever reason—perhaps boredom, antsiness after being away from her friends for two days, or perhaps having gestated deeply on the matter for two years, or, more likely, a combination of these and other reasons—she agreed to *possibly* go out the next day, the last day, though only for a very little while.

I was, of course, exultant. The snow was already beginning to fall. I cleaned my grandfather's old rifle and showed her how to use it; we practiced with its "false" trigger: the first 90 percent of the squeeze mushy, but then the calming firmness that indicated the last 10 percent—the final breath, final thought—was at the ready.

We did not snap the firing pin, nor did we shoot a live round, for I remembered how loud the rifle was the first time I had shot it, at an older age than she, and I did not want her being flinchy, nor did I want to give her any possible reason for changing her mind again.

I went to bed disbelieving my great luck—to be a father to these two girls is more than I could ever possibly deserve or hope for, but to then be able to take one of them out into the woods, into the valley I love, to go on our first hunt, felt as if I had been wandering in a field of happiness and then had fallen, as if through a trapdoor, into greater happiness.

I awakened early on that last morning, my blood afizz with winter insomnia, and wrote from about four until daylight, and then woke Mary Katherine. That had been part of the bargain, to which I had willingly agreed: letting her sleep in and get her teenager's rest. Certainly it's much finer to be out in the woods before first light, but to tell the truth I was enjoying it at least as much sitting there by the woodstove while everyone else slept, warm and dry, in my house over the Thanksgiving holidays and knowing that I would, soon enough—after thirteen years of waiting—be walking out into the woods to go hunting, deer hunting, with my older daughter, as my father had once gone out into the woods with me, as his father had once first gone out into the woods with him, as had my grandfather's father once—and so on, perhaps all the way back to the source of the time of man.

I was not in a rush. It was very calm and wonderful, standing there by the window listening to the fire, and watching the snow coming down, and listening also to the good silence of everyone else in the house asleep at such a fine time of day, over the holiday.

In my morning's work—which on the best mornings, as any writer knows, is a kind of deep meditation, which, after an hour or two, can approach the realm of prayer or dialogue with a further, other world, nearing whispers, or encountering the space and silence preceding those whispers, if such exist—it had begun to occur to me that we might be fortunate enough to find a deer.

That was neither my goal nor my expectation—all I wanted was to walk quietly in the woods with my older daughter, during hunting season, and to hope and watch for a deer: *to go hunting*—but that morning, as I had worked on a manuscript, on a passage that involved the paths of travelers crossing over into unmapped territory, a metaphor began to develop in my mind, if not on the page or yet in the real world, in which the conditions were right—given the new snow and the rut—for travelers such as ourselves to be rewarded with a little miracle, or maybe even a big one, if we dared to hope and believe.

No real matter. I already had all in the world that I wanted.

It was strange, packing two of everything, even for so short a jaunt as we were preparing to take: a thermos of hot chocolate with two cups; two blaze-orange camouflage jackets, two pair of dry socks, two stocking caps. And as we drove to the trailhead of the place I planned to hunt—a place where I knew there were several deer in a beautiful old larch forest—the effervescence of my blood continued to shine and shimmer. I do not think our frail bodies could withstand every day being like that one, in which nearly all that one has asked or hoped for is delivered and in which everything beyond that deliverance—unasked for, and unexpected—is gravy.

We parked, fastened our gaiters, got out, closing the doors quietly, and started up the steep trail, walking on brilliant new snow, with more coming down around us. After a lifetime of hunting by myself, it was quite a different thing to be looking at the mountain not just with my eyes, but also those of another, and for another. Whispering to her, now and again, and pointing out the direction of the breeze and the bark-rubbed saplings where the bucks had been at work. Complimenting her quiet footsteps and pointing out the old tracks, as well as those from earlier in the morning. Entering with her that electric, other world, as if passing through a looking glass: and on the other side of it, with her, now.

Anything could happen. That's one of the greatest things about hunting this northern valley: in the next step, or the next, we could see absolutely anything, or the sign of that thing's passage. A great grey owl, or the track of a late-to-hibernate black bear, or maybe even a grizzly. A herd of elk, a lion, a lynx, anything. A deer.

We walked slowly and carefully, ascending to a shelf where there was etched so great a stippling of that morning's tracks that it reminded me of the trident calligraphy of shorebirds on the beach. We had been walking only about fifteen minutes, and I was looking for a good place to sit and watch. It was important not to overdo it, this first time: to not push on to the next horizon, and then beyond.

The snow was lessening, and a north wind was picking up, scrubbing the fog and rime from the forest and cleaning out our lungs, our blood, our hearts. It was that wintertime north breeze from the forest that is so clear, and wedges and puzzle-pieces of blue sky were appearing now, and the openings in the clouds were allowing that buttery-rich yellow-gold winter sunlight to plunge down through the old larch forest—their branches bare in winter, shrouded now only in moss and lichen—and in one such column of light, I saw the head and ears of a doe lying down behind a fallen log, resting. She was bedded by a rushing little creek and was as illuminated, at two or three hundred yards' distance, as if a spotlight had been fixed upon her. The new snow around her sparkled in that rare vertical plume of sunlight, making it look frosted. She did not see us and seemed extraordinarily becalmed, as animals often do on certain peaceful or beautiful mornings.

We watched her for a while, and it was an interesting and curious whispered conversation I had with Mary Katherine, trying to explain to her the inexplicable: that I did not care for us to hunt this doe, for any number of reasons, of which the beauty and creekside tranquility were only one, but that it might be fun to try to sneak in closer to her and wait and watch to see if a buck might be nearby, or might even come in to her.

And as we were watching, a young-of-the-year fawn, a five-month-old, popped up from behind the same log, and, made frisky by the same cold clean air that was filling us, he ran in two quick circles around his mother. More columns of sunlight were spreading into the forest now, and the whole sky above was going to blue, up on the shelf, with the fog being swept southward and filling the lower trough of the valley. The fawn pranced and whirled, bucking and twisting like a tiny rodeo horse, trying to throw some equally tiny, and unseen, rider: and it was more gravy, this opportunity, or lesson, to show her right from the start that hunting, like some lives—not enough, in my opinion—consists of a significant amount of intuition; that when one is fully engaged, one has greater authority, not less, to operate by one's senses and instincts. You're not always right, but you are sometimes, and it was gratifying to see the previously inexplicable, that which was not quite able to be articulated, so clearly explicated, as if in the next breath, and by the breath of another, about why it had not felt right to hunt this bedded doe.

We crept, crawled, stalked toward the recumbent doe and her goofy fawn, always keeping a big tree or a tangle of fallen lodgepole between us and her. The north wind was in our face, protecting our scent completely, and it seemed that the sound of the creek, along which we were creeping, and beside which she was resting, had mesmerized her.

We crept to within sixty or seventy yards and then hunkered down behind a random corral of blowdown: as if laborers had begun building a cabin or other structure, setting the first two or three courses before being called away for some little irrelevance—a glass of water, a cup of coffee—from which they had never returned.

For me, everything is an equal part of the hunt, and all of it is wonderful—boiling the water for hot chocolate and making sure we had our licenses, etc. were no different from us tucking in tight against that fallen natural corral of logs and breathing smoke plumes of frost as we watched the doe and her fawn—but I noticed that for Mary Katherine, this new part was quite a bit different, which of course made sense. For me, it was the point where she might soon lift the rifle and put the scope on the heart of a deer.

We were hidden well, a near-perfect set-up, and existing deliciously, intensely, in the moment. Much later I would allow myself the thought, the pondering, of how long ago the wind had passed through that had tipped over this matchstick arrangement of lodgepole—from the looks of them, it could easily have been thirteen years ago, or even longer—that gust of wind preparing a place, some distance into the future, for Mary Katherine, even before she was here—but there by the creek, I was thinking none of these things, was only tucked in with her against the housestacking of logs, watching and waiting.

In less than a minute, another deer appeared, a nice young four-point buck, trotting in from stage left, just as I had whispered to her might happen. I tensed with excitement, pleasure, hope, disbelief, gratitude, hunger, desire—the whole complex and utterly specific, utterly inexplicable chain reaction of responses known only to a hunter when his or her quarry presents itself—and I felt Mary Katherine, beside me, respond in the same way.

It's not a question of right or wrong—there is and should be no set prescription for responses to the human experience—but I find it hard to imagine that almost anyone in such a setting would not likewise tense with anticipation, joy, wonder, and excitement, for it was not so long ago at all that this, as much as anything, was the main currency of human existence, and the human condition.

It's fine, I suppose, for individuals to have lost such connection or rootstock—there's no stopping time, and no stopping change—and it would have been all right with me if Mary Katherine was one of those people who, for whatever reason, no longer possessed, nor even understood, that connection. But this was what I wanted to show her—to lead her right up to the edge of it—and it pleased me, and only surprised me a little, to see that, given this baseline shared experience, she felt pretty much the same jolt that I did.

Anything from here on was more gravy. Nothing but marvel, nothing but miracle.

The buck stopped, posing—angled forty-five degrees toward us, an impossible shot at any distance, and with parts of his body obscured also by trees—and gazed for long moments at the bedded doe, who turned her head to look back at him as if—or so it seemed to me—trying to pretend she had not known he was in the neighborhood.

I whispered to Mary Katherine to lift the rifle and place it over the top log, or between two logs, and to find the buck in the scope, and to be ready, should he move forward and place himself in a position where she could take a clean shot. He was about eighty or ninety yards out.

Mary Katherine couldn't find him in the scope—so many trees, so much snow on the ground, so much sky; who among us had not known that frustration of seeing a thing with bare eyes, but then not being able to find it with the scope, the instrument that was specifically designed to aid, not hinder, our vision?—but it was good practice for her, and we were in no rush, for I was beginning to perceive already that this deer was intended for us, for her. We—she—might not be successful in taking it, but we had not come to this place, this random corral on the first hunt and the last day of the season, to not be presented with a chance, as long as we kept up our end of the bargain.

After more gazing—more be-rutted mesmerization—the buck suddenly lowered his head and charged not the doe, but the fawn. Whether it was a mock charge or the real thing, I couldn't be sure; it looked real to me, and I think it did to the fawn, too, for it stumbled over logs trying to get out of the way, zigging and zagging and tail-flagging almost as if at play, and yet using the scattered windthrow for an escape route, which made me think perhaps it was not play.

The fawn, the yearling, came straight at us, eyes wild—*thundering*, if so small an animal can be said to thunder—and was just on the verge of running right over the top of us before it saw some small movement—perhaps our own eyes widening—and veered away, kicking up a spray of snow as it bounded over the brook, which was so narrow that Mary Katherine or I could have similarly cleared it.

It's always the problem with getting in too close on a herd of deer or elk: once one of them discovers you, even the best-laid plans will usually begin to crumble, with that one discoverer—be it doe, buck, or even clueless yearling—huffing and snorting and blowing your cover. I was a little discouraged that already we had come to this part of the hunt; though thrilled, too, that we had seen so much, and in such a short time, and on so short a venture. As if somehow I had been gifted, some strange and wonderful recompense for all the countless hours spent slogging, crawling, sliding, trudging, lost and beaten, in which no game at all had been sighted. As if all that failure—or perceived failure—had merely been preparation for the summary deliverance of this luck, this grace.

The yearling chose not to stick around to blow our cover. Wisely, I think, he added the threats of the day—an angry older buck, and hunters crouched with rifle raised—and decided the heck with warning the others, and if they didn't want him around anyway, fine, let them figure it out on their own.

Amazingly, the scene before us settled back down: adjusted itself to even more of a wintertime picture-pastoral scene of classic holiday tranquility. The lissome doe rose to her feet and cantered off a short distance, looked back at the buck, and then loped across the creek herself, farther upstream, and I thought for a moment that she too was panicked: but perhaps the buck would remain oblivious, and as he stood there, trying to figure things out, I continued to try to assist Mary Katherine in locating him in the scope, though to no avail.

Then he began moving, his winter-gray body passing slowly through the trees, antlers gleaming, and possessing a different, more significant musculature than the doe.

"I think we're going to get a shot at him," I whispered. Mary Katherine shifted, lifted her eye from the scope, saw him, then put her eye to the scope and found him. "I see him," she said.

"If he stops, and you're comfortable with the shot, take it," I said. "You don't have to if you don't want to. But if you want to take this deer, he's a nice one, and this is a good hunt."

She tensed, stilled herself, and I could tell that was her answer, and slowly, I put my fingers to my ears.

The buck did not stop, however, and disappeared into the trees that lined either side of the brook.

Still, it wasn't over. He was clearly tracking the doe and yearling, and it was possible, I knew, he would walk right into our laps.

"Come with me," I whispered, noting an even more strategic hollow into which we could nestle ourselves, one with better crossbar-spars for resting her rifle. A perfect brace and a perfect set-up, whether the buck continued downstream toward the tangle in which we were hunkered, or—best of all—crossed the creek and moved out into the fairly open stand of mature larch, where he would be hugely exposed, and even closer. The perfect thing would be for him to saunter through that beautiful open forest, visible all the way—his eyes trained for the gone-away doe and also watching his footing amidst lodgepole—to a fairly open point on a little knoll, about fifty yards to our right, where I could, if he was still walking, give a little grunt on the deer call, at which point—becalmed as he was now—he might turn his head to look in the direction of the sound and pause broadside, searching for the thing he had been looking for, the thing upon which he had been focusing. And then—if it was a clean good shot—he would know nothing.

I explained all this to Mary Katherine, pointing and gesturing and whispering quickly as we belly-crawled to our newer, more secure spot. Excited but also calmly confident, I had the sense, the image, that our tiny sounds were obscured by the riffle of the brook—that the buck was crossing the creek, and that in a short few moments we would see him appear on the other side, in that more open area, as if he had walked onto another stage.

No sooner had we gotten settled than indeed we saw a deer enter this other, more open stage—but it was the doe.

She walked among the giant trees, exposing herself almost the entire way—and Mary Katherine asked if she could shoot this deer.

"No," I said, tenderhearted, "she may still be with that yearling. Let's wait on the buck. I think he'll be coming."

The doe walked on, then, aiming for that little knoll, where—as if we had already seen it in a vision—she paused, then disappeared over the back side of it.

Now the buck came into that clearing, following the doe's trail as if fastened to her by an invisible packstring. He stopped at one point sixty yards out—"Take the shot if you want, and if you're comfortable," I whispered, to which Mary Katherine whispered, "I see him, I see him," and again, I covered my ears—but then he started walking once more, and I felt Mary Katherine relax with disappointment, though still eager, still ready.

"Don't worry," I said. "You'll get another chance. He'll cross right through there, and I'll blow on the grunt tube, and when I do, you be ready, because he'll stop. You don't have to shoot, but if you do, hold steady, exhale, and squeeze cleanly."

We waited, watching the deer cross his final steps toward that place to which, if you are so inclined to think about such things, he had been striding for forty-eight years, or for all time: and we watched, together, as if counting his final paces, as he moved nearer that spot where I would blow on the grunt tube and, distracted from one purpose, he would stop and turn and look in our direction.

Mary Katherine's and my breath rose in twin vapors. The buck kept moving through the old larch forest. Soon his path would carry him beyond us. I raised the grunt tube to my lips and blew, and—again as if we, with our imagination and desire, or something else with similar design and desire, had planned such—the buck stopped broadside in the open and looked in our direction.

"That's a good shot," I whispered. "Take it if you want it." And once again, I covered my ears, and watched.

I had not expected her to hit it. I had expected her to shoot high, or low, or not at all. I was delighted to hear the concussive sea-roar for which I had been waiting and, despite being hopeful and having planned for success, was astounded to see the deer hop hunch-backed, all four feet off the ground like a bull in the rodeo, and then take off running.

"I missed him," she lamented. "I don't know how, but I missed him."

I laughed. "No, you got him," I said. I pointed to the knoll. "He ran around behind that and then fell down stone dead. You'll see."

She shook her head. "I missed him. I can't believe it," she said. "I missed him."

"No," I said, "I guarantee, you hit him."

She wanted to get up then and go see, but I explained to her that we had to wait. Generally an hour, I told her, but with so much snow down, we could cut it to a half-hour wait here.

It was a pleasure to sit quietly with her and replay the hunt in each intimate detail, and to praise and brag on her, and to see her pride and pleasure at such discussion, leavened as it was, however, by doubt.

It was a wonderful microcosm of our life. She was in a hurry to go ascertain her success, or lack of success, while I was delighted to be enjoying the moment, savoring that required waiting time. She was in a hurry to grow up, while I wanted to wait quietly just a little bit longer. One more year, one more month, one more week: this half hour, this moment, *anything*.

We sat and talked quietly, until we began to shiver. I kept telling her not to worry, and she kept worrying. It was a good transition time, I realized, for her to adjust to the reality of what had just transpired, and her participation—that she had indeed just killed an animal, which, as millions of people have pointed out, is not at all the same thing as walking into the store and purchasing it.

We got up and walked slowly, quietly, to the place where the bullet had intercepted the deer. I purposely brought her in on its backtrail, so she could see in the snow the before-and-after of the deer walking, and then running, and the scatter of loose gray hair on the snow, and the blood sign that indicated, like a signature, the fact that we would soon be claiming this deer—but when we came to that divot-spot of hump-shouldered sky-leap, I could find neither hair nor blood, only tossed-up black earth and humus from the sharp-hooved bolt, and Mary Katherine despaired, believing in her teen heart, and not at all for the first time, that I was wrong and she was right.

"It's got to be here," I said, still confident, though I have to say, I went from 100 percent to maybe 99 percent. I followed the tracks a little farther and finally found a few drops of blood, and four or five loose hairs. "There," I said, though I was disappointed by how little there was. What if she had only creased his back, barely even breaking the skin? And after I had assured her otherwise. Perhaps there is no guide who has never been in this heart-sinking position, but it was my first time.

We followed the tracks carefully, quietly, in case the deer, only lightly wounded, or perhaps not at all, should leap up in front of us. I showed Mary Katherine how important it was when tracking a deer to not step in its tracks: that you always needed to preserve the option of being able to come back and reinterpret things. That you could easily—and often did—get thrown off-track, and that when that happened, you would have to circle back and start over.

I continued to be discouraged by how little blood there was and by how unhurried the buck's gait was—the tracks seemed to indicate he was in control of his carriage—and by how far apart the blood spots were. I worried to myself what would happen when we ran out of blood spots, and when the buck's tracks merged with those of other deer.

Then the blood spots disappeared completely—after only twenty or thirty yards, we were tracking clean again—and I cautioned Mary Katherine to stop and look out into the old forest to see if the buck might be standing at the far side, looking back at us. It had happened that way with me many times, with deer as well as elk—the snort, the flag of tail, the unharmed animal curious and not particularly wary, during the rut, watching the hunter approach, and with the hunter's eyes fixed on the ground, rather than on the path ahead—and although I was beginning to worry we might not find this deer, or that the odds were becoming longer with each step, it pleased me to realize that everything I was telling her, this fine last-day morning, was new information to her. It made me feel useful. The only thing now that could make the morning feel finer was to come upon the miracle of the buck piled up a short distance away.

After forty yards, we came to an ice-bed where he had lain briefly, waiting quietly, while we had been waiting on the other side of the hill. There was very little blood there and I felt less assured than ever.

It's all a puzzle, all but an assemblage of pieces, always. Had the buck run those thirty or forty yards, knelt down, then leapt up at our approach? Or had he only lain there for mere seconds before jumping up and staggering on now, thrashing his way toward that final place that in his animal mind was surely only just a little farther on?

I stopped, trying to slow time down—trying to fully inhabit and remember the moment, being in the woods on the last day of the season with my older daughter on our first hunt—and saw the buck piled up in more lodgepole not another fifteen yards away. Mary Katherine was still staring glumly at the vacant ice-bed.

"Follow his tracks," I said. "Keep following his tracks." I was tempted to say *just a little farther*, but didn't.

And carefully, cautiously, she led the way: head down, moving from track to track—there was more blood now, a lot of blood, and broken logs and branches indicating a heaviness of passage, and I understood that all this had transpired in mere seconds, following her shot: that it was only with our cautious walking that we were seeming to attenuate it.

She walked almost right up to him—was within only about seven or eight yards when she looked up and saw his long body lying stretched out over the fallen lodgepole, as if still in mid-leap, and with the antlers still held aloft, rather than side-tipped, tilting, as with many fallen deer.

We approached him quietly, respectfully. I looked around at the day and said, "Thank you woods, thank you valley, thank you deer, thank you Mary Katherine, thank you *everything*," and then we examined the animal and remembered the hunt a little further. I took some pictures of her with the animal, and then we set about cleaning it, and as we did so, I pointed out the organs, biology lab writ large.

She helped, and afterward we wiped our hands in the snow, and then began dragging the deer out, and what a delight it was to sled, me with my aging body, that deer through the woods and over the fallen logs and down the mountain. What a delight, an honor, to feel so acutely, and in such celebration, my own mortality: a task that was once insignificant to me now ponderous and significant. I, too, stumbled and tripped, and stopped often to rest, but was able to gather my breath then and keep going.

The ravens saw us moving through the woods and began to call and follow, and I imagined how timeless and normal it must have seemed, from their perspective—just two more hunters who had been fortunate enough to find a deer. They cawed and called to one another, wheeling and backtracking our tracks, to that point where we had cleaned the deer.

Did they know anything, I wondered, of the extra fire and joy in my heart, the pride and strange peace? Or were they simply calling, was it only another meal for them?

I wanted them to know differently. I wanted them to know how this one was different. I wanted the whole world to know, but it was just me and Mary Katherine, moving quietly through the snowy forest, with everything around us and in us ancient and new.

CREDITS

"My Naturalist Mother," *Texas Monthly*, July 2010 (as "Wild at Heart")

"Records," *Sports Afield*, December 1994

"The Other Fort Worth Basses," *Texas Monthly*, November 1991

"On Willow Creek," *Los Angeles Times Sunday Magazine*, November 28, 1993

"Deer Camp," *Texas Monthly*, November 2011 (as "Eat, Prey, Love")

"This Year's Hunt," *Texas Parks & Wildlife*, December 2004 (as "Outsmarted by Turkeys")

"The Deer Pasture," *Field & Stream*, November 2009

"The Silent Language," previously unpublished

"A Texas Childhood," portions published in *Texas Monthly*, March 2003, and *DoubleTake*, Spring 2003

"Colter's Creek Buck," portions published in *Texas Parks & Wildlife*, January 2005 (as "The Second Hunt") and *Texas Monthly*, January 2011 ("Stuck Truck")

"Aoudads," *Texas Parks & Wildlife*, November 2003 (as "Return to the Deer Pasture")

"Mary Katherine's First Deer," *Gray's Sporting Journal*, September/October 2008